FOR YOUR PROFESSIONAL BOOKSHELF
from
ENERGY PSYCHOLOGY PRESS

The Human Hologram
Living Your Life in Harmony with the Unified Field
By Dr. Robin Kelly

A London-trained physician presents evidence that our physical bodies are perpetually being formed upon an invisible field of information, and that as our consciousness interacts with that field, we can optimize our health.

Softcover, 6" x 9", 256 pages $16.95

Soul Medicine
Awakening Your Inner Blueprint for Abundant Health and Energy
By Norman Shealy, MD, PhD, and Dawson Church, PhD

A neurosurgeon and founder of the American Holistic Medical Association, Shealy teams up with health researcher Dawson Church to present the latest studies showing the healing effects of energy, intention and consciousness.

Softcover, 6" x 9", 296 pages $17.95

Heal Your Mind, Rewire Your Brain
Applying the Exciting New Science of Brain Plasticity for Creativity, Peace and Presence
By Patt Lind-Kyle, MA

Applies the latest exciting scientific discoveries in a practical, step-by-step program that literally rewires neural connections in the brain for greater happiness.

Hardcover, 6" x 9", 32 Illustrations, 253 pages $26.95

Creating Healing Relationships
Professional Standards for Energy Therapy Practitioners
By Dorothea Hover-Kramer, EdD, RN, DCEP

Written by the co-founder of ACEP, the professional organization for Energy Psychology, this is the first book to seriously address the need for professional standards in the rapidly growing field of energy healing.

Hardcover, 6" x 9", 256 pages $35

Body Eloquence
The Power of Myth and Story to Awaken the Body's Energies
By Nancy Mellon, MFT with Ashley Ramsden

Have you ever had an ache or pain, and wished your body could talk to you and tell you what was wrong? Drawing from mythology, medicine, biology and energetic healing, this book shows the messages that our organs are communicating to us.

Trade Paper, 7" x 10", 15 Illustrations, 260 pages $18.95

Energy Healer's Ethics Handbook
By David Feinstein, PhD, with Donna Eden

This comprehensive, case-oriented guide allows veterans of the field and newcomers alike to work through a wide range of ethical dilemmas before they arise, helping you to prevent professional errors that could hurt you, your clients, and your practice.

Hardcover, 6" x 9", 210 pages $39

ENERGY PSYCHOLOGY PRESS

Order now at EnergyPsychologyPress.com

Energy Psychology
Theory, Research, and Treatment

A Journal of the National Institute for Integrative Healthcare (NIIH.org)

www.EnergyPsychologyJournal.org

Energy Psychology: Theory, Research, and Treatment is a peer-reviewed professional journal dedicated to reporting developments in the field of energy psychology (EP) that are of interest to health care professionals and researchers. It contains original empirical research into the efficacy of EP methods; theoretical, experimental, and basic science papers illuminating the mechanisms of action of EP; clinical insights on the application of EP to various populations, and interfaces with other interventions; book reviews, and abstracts published in other journals that are of relevance to the EP field. Its goal is to further the development of EP as an evidence-based method in the healing sciences. It conforms to the editorial, stylistic, and ethical standards of the American Psychological Association (APA.org).

Energy Psychology: Theory, Research, and Treatment (ISSN 1949-6575) is published biannually (November and May) by Energy Psychology Press, PO Box 442, Fulton, CA 95439. For customer service or advertising information, contact 707-237-6951 or energypsychologypress@gmail.com.

POSTMASTER: Send address changes to: *Energy Psychology* journal, PO Box 442, Fulton, CA 95439.

YEARLY SUBSCRIPTION RATES: $49.95 per issue, $99.95 per year.

AUTHOR ENQUIRIES: Submit paper copies of proposed papers to *Energy Psychology* journal, PO Box 442, Fulton, CA 95439. Include an e-mail address and phone number for the corresponding author. All submissions should conform fully to the requirements of the *Publication Manual of the American Psychological Association,* sixth edition. Include a cover letter as specified on the "Submissions" link at www.EnergyPsychologyJournal.org, and manuscripts should be prepared in conformity with the other standards published there. Acceptance or rejection will be made via e-mail; paper copies will not be returned. If a submission is accepted for peer review, all subsequent contact will occur via e-mail. Deadline for Spring issue submissions is Jan 15 of each year, and July 15 for Fall issue.

REPRINTS: Back issues are available for $49.95. Reprint ordering information may be found at www.EnergyPsychologyPress.com. To order 100 or more copies of a particular paper, contact energypsychologypress@gmail.com.

Contents

May 2023 • Volume 15, Number 1

About

ENERGY PSYCHOLOGY: THEORY, RESEARCH, AND TREATMENT

Energy Psychology (EP) is an evolving and maturing field that is rapidly meeting the standards of proof for "evidence-based" practice. Studies of EP have demonstrated its efficacy for a wide range of psychological and physical problems, from phobias to pain to posttraumatic stress disorder. EP is now being researched in hospital systems such as Britain's National Health Service (NHS), large private hospital chains such as Kaiser Permanente and Sutter Health, and the United States Department of Veterans Affairs (VA). By providing a rigorous, high-quality, peer-reviewed platform for the publication of research results, theory, and clinical insights, this journal provides a forum for the exchange of the key discoveries and ideas that drive the EP field forward.

—Dawson Church, PhD
Editor, *Energy Psychology: Theory, Research, and Treatment*

The journal publishes work in the following areas:

EDITORIAL ESSAYS include guest editorials from some of the best thinkers and researchers in EP today;

ORIGINAL RESEARCH provides empirical evidence for various EP methods;

CLINICAL REPORTS describe the use of EP with challenging conditions and specific populations and provide guidance for empirical research;

INTERFACES WITH OTHER THERAPIES show how EP is typically used in conjunction with other methods, such as cognitive behavior therapy (CBT), mindfulness therapy, addiction counseling, sports psychology, medicine, energy medicine, meditation, and life coaching;

REVIEW ARTICLES are theoretical papers, literature reviews, reports of innovations, and analyses that explore issues from the professional condition of EP to the physiological mechanisms of action of EP;

BOOK REVIEWS cover new and classic EP-related titles;

ABSTRACTS published in other journals relevant to EP are reprinted.

EDITORIAL BOARD

Living the Flow

Dawson Church

Mihaly Csikszentmihalyi, PhD, University of Chicago psychologist and founder of the Quality of Life Research Center, was known as the "father of flow" for his pioneering work in the field of autotelic experience, or flow. Since his book *Beyond Boredom and Anxiety: Experiencing Flow in Work and Play* came out in 1975, interest in and research on the flow state have grown exponentially.

The flow state is its own reward. Autotelic is from the Greek *auto* ("self") and *telos* ("goal or purpose"), meaning activities done for their own sake. Alternate terms for this state are being in "the zone," peak performance, and optimal performance. In terms of brain function, the flow state is called "transient hypo-frontality." The "transient" part means that the state is temporary. "Hypo" is jargon for reduced function. "Frontality" refers to the prefrontal cortex, the executive region of the brain's cortex. Among other functions, it constructs our sense of self (with all our obsessions about perfection, status, and performance) and plans for the future. When it goes "hypo" during the flow state, all that busy "monkey mind" activity quiets down.

Csikszentmihalyi defined flow as "a state in which people are so involved in an activity that nothing else seems to matter; the experience is so enjoyable that people will continue to do it even at great cost, for the sheer sake of doing it" (Steimer, 2021). The word "flow" as applied to this peak state arose from some of Csikszentmihalyi's interview subjects who described the state as like being carried along by a water current (Steimer, 2021).

There are eight characteristics of the flow state, according to Csikszentmihalyi (1990):

1. Complete concentration
2. Clear goals and immediate feedback
3. Speeding up or slowing down of time
4. Intrinsically rewarding
5. Effortlessness and ease
6. Balance between challenge and skills
7. Merged action and awareness; lack of self-conscious thought
8. Feeling of control over the task

Steven Kotler, a prominent flow researcher and author of *The Art of Impossible: A Peak Performance Primer*, among other books, is one of the researchers who built on Csikszentmihalyi's work. He states: "Our research shows that when skillfully deployed…, these 'characteristics' consistently generate more flow and are better classified as 'triggers'" (Kotler, 2020, 2023a).

The concept of triggers is compelling as people in all fields and walks of life seek ways to induce the flow state for optimum performance. Inducing "group flow" is of special interest to people for whom team performance matters, from athletes to entrepreneurs to administrators to family members. Expanding on Csikszentmihalyi's list, Keith Sawyer, a psychologist at the University of North Carolina, points to 10 triggers that induce group flow (Kotler, 2020):

1. Shared goals
2. Fully attentive listening
3. "Yes, and" language in interactions, building on rather than being combative
4. Complete concentration and focus in the present moment
5. A sense of control and, at the same time, flexibility
6. Blending egos; willingness to submerge one's ego needs in group needs
7. Equal participation
8. Familiarity with each member of the group
9. Constant communication ("a group version of immediate feedback")
10. Shared risk ("everyone has some skin in the game")

By implementing these qualities in your group activity, whatever it may be, your group is more likely to experience the magic of flow, when what you produce as a group exceeds normal expectations and the creation of the product is far more enjoyable and even exciting than work produced during a non-flow state.

Kotler has gone further in exploring traits that can help induce the immensely satisfying feeling of flow, when everything just goes right and feels effortless. He identifies four more triggers, as revealed by research into flow (Kotler, 2020):

1. High consequences (physical, mental, social, emotional, creative, and/or other risk)
2. Deep embodiment ("the engagement of multiple sensory streams at once, learning through doing")
3. Rich environment (novelty, complexity, and unpredictability)
4. Creativity ("specifically, pattern recognition, or the linking together of new ideas")

Typically, we might regard novelty, complexity, and unpredictability as reasons for fear. What research is telling us now, though, is we can change our perspective in how we regard these qualities and embrace them as keys for entering the state of flow, which naturally leaves fear behind.

Kotler's personal favorite flow-inducing sport is skiing. His research has shown that if you challenge yourself on a ski slope that slightly exceeds your comfort level, you can trigger flow. His book *Gnar Country: Growing Old, Staying Rad* (Kotler, 2023b), describes his attempts to learn a challenging new style of skiing—at an age 20 years older than that at which it's normally considered achievable.

I've interviewed Kotler several times, and while I'm not a skier, we share a passion for mountain biking, a warm-weather alternative. Once or twice a day, summer or winter, rain or shine, I take my mountain bike for a spin through the steepest hills I can find nearby. I've found that pushing my limits each ride puts me into flow.

Kotler has measured the amount of challenge required to stimulate flow. Too big a stretch, like exceeding your past performance by 25%, is more likely to produce stress than exhilaration. His research team has found that 4% is the magic number. Make the task just 4% outside your comfort zone, and you trigger flow. So I try zipping around hairpin bends on my bike just 4% tighter or 4% faster than before. Flow squeezes out the worries of my mind; when you're taking a switchback at 25 miles per hour on a powdery dirt track, there's no room for error and even less for reflective mental chatter. The prefrontal cortex quiets down and you slip completely into the present moment.

Flow is its own reward. At the same time, it raises productivity and satisfaction significantly. Building flow triggers into your tasks, endeavors, exercise, and goals will increase the amount of time you spend in that fulfilling state of present-moment existence.

References

Csikszentmihalyi, M. (1975). *Beyond boredom and anxiety: Experiencing flow in work and play*. Jossey-Bass.

——. (1990). *Flow: The psychology of optimal experience*. Harper & Row.

Kotler, S. (2020). *Frequently asked questions on flow*. Retrieved from https://www.stevenkotler.com/rabbit-hole/frequently-asked-questions-on-flow

——. (2023a). *The art of impossible: A peak performance primer*. Harper.

——. (2023b). *Gnar country: Growing old, staying rad*. Harper.

Steimer, S. (2021). Mihaly Csikszentmihalyi, pioneering psychologist and "father of flow," 1934–2021. *UChicago news*. Retrieved from https://news.uchicago.edu/story/mihaly-csikszentmihalyi-pioneering-psychologist-and-father-flow-1934-2021

Energy Psychology, Bilateral Stimulation, and Mindful Breathing for Trauma and Chronic Pain: A Theoretical Framework and Case History

Gloria N. Valdivieso, Weston, Florida, USA

Abstract

Research and anecdotal evidence from clinical practice suggest high comorbidity between trauma and chronic pain. Unresolved trauma can generate anxiety and dissociation, both associated with chronic pain. Even though there are proven interventions to treat trauma and pain individually, efforts to treat the comorbidity and complexity of these two disorders on a combined basis are not yet fully explored. This article introduces a protocol that blends aspects of four evidence-based interventions. These interventions are Emotional Freedom Techniques (EFT), bilateral stimulation (BLS) as used in Eye Movement Desensitization and Reprocessing (EMDR), Wholistic Hybrid derived from EMDR and EFT (WHEE), and mindful breathing (MB) to treat traumatized individuals that exhibit chronic pain. The combined protocol uses the benefits of each intervention. The technique involves tapping on the eight meridian points designated in the EFT Basic Recipe while using a Neurotek pulser to generate BLS, after a "dialogue with the body symptoms" extracted from the WHEE method to uncover the traumatic memories or negative beliefs associated with pain. To close the session, the Quick Coherence Technique, a heart-focused MB exercise developed by the HeartMath Institute, is utilized to further help individuals with self-regulation and increased appreciation of their bodies. This article explains how the technique is performed through a six-step sample methodology and what the potential of its combined effectiveness can look like in a case history. The subject of the clinical case study profited in reducing his chronic pain by combining mindful breathing and EFT as the more gentle, non-retraumatizing, and distress-reducing techniques with the recovery of repressed memories via BLS and the inner-body dialogue of WHEE. Given the comorbidity of trauma and chronic pain and the lack of integrative interventions, additional scholarly inquiry into healing the various complex issues of these disorders is essential to develop. Refining the evidence on such blended methods should be the focus of future work to encourage practitioners' training and increase service delivery.

Keywords: trauma, chronic pain, dissociation, EFT, EMDR, mindful breathing, bilateral stimulation, BLS, WHEE, HeartMath, blended, combined, interventions

Gloria N. Valdivieso, DSW, LCSW, is a licensed clinical social worker in private practice and the clinical director at Care Counselors, a trauma-informed clinic that specializes in serving adolescents and adults that have experienced trauma in their lives. **Correspondence:** Gloria Valdivieso, 2807 Kinsington Circle, Weston, FL 33332 USA; email: carecounselors4u@gmail.com. **Disclosure:** The procedures and modalities outlined in this article are used in the author's therapy practice. The author receives a fee for a general therapy session, however, no extra fees are charged for the inclusion of these modalities.

The study of trauma and the association of traumatic events with the development of posttraumatic stress disorder (PTSD) and other mental health conditions has been ample in the past few decades. There are multiple definitions of trauma; however, this article will use the Substance Abuse and Mental Health Services Administration (SAMHSA) definition, as it presents a comprehensive representation of trauma as follows:

"Individual trauma results from an event, series of events, or a set of circumstances experienced by an individual as physically or emotionally harmful or life-threatening and has lasting adverse effects on the individual's functioning and mental, physical, social, emotional, or spiritual well-being" (SAMHSA, 2014, p.7).

Pain is vital to our survival, allowing us to adapt to our environment, alerting us to the potential danger of tissue damage, and encouraging us into action to reduce additional harm and begin a course of recovery (Wall, 1979). Initially, pain was theorized as only a sensory experience stemming from a stimulus of particular high threshold receptors resulting from physical injury or progressive disease (Asmundson & Katz, 2009). Current models understand that pain is more than just a sensation but rather a complex physical and emotional experience that produces devastating negative impacts in every aspect of life created by sensory, psychological, and social influences (Asmundson et al., 2004).

Even if pain has a clear physical origin, there is always a psychological component that makes the pain more or less tolerable than it should be (Benor, 2008). For example, after an injury, a person might feel depressed because they might have the perception of being less able, feebler, or declining in age. As a result, these negative feelings and beliefs might make the pain worse. There is significant research linking chronic pain with psychiatric illnesses such as substance abuse, depression, and anxiety disorders (Asmundson et al., 2004; Peres et al., 2009; Roy-Byrne et al., 2008; Sareen et al., 2005). Viewing pain through a holistic healing model assumes that the intervention must be geared toward healing the person that has the pain and not the pain that the person has. Additionally, a holistic way of addressing pain involves a subjective experience of every person in interaction with themselves, in their relationships, with their environment, and in their spiritual connections (Benor, 2008). This article will use different labels (such as somatization, somatoform disorders, and somatic symptoms) to describe symptoms of pain that cannot be explained in terms of a traditionally demarcated medical disease.

There is considerable evidence of the relationship between trauma and chronic pain (Beckham et al., 1997; McFarlane et al., 1994; Shepherd et al., 2007). Clinical practice and research suggest that chronic pain and traumatic stress co-occur at a high rate and may negatively affect the course of each other (Asmundson et al., 2002). It is common for patients who suffer from chronic pain to describe multiple levels of distress, including PTSD symptomatology (Peres et al., 2009). Furthermore, researchers in a variety of disciplines, including psychology, medicine, and epidemiology, have found this relationship to be present; however, the lack of cohesiveness among fields has limited the use of their findings (Kendall-Tackett & Klest, 2009).

Methods: A Brief on New Evidence-Based Interventions

Cognitive processing, also called top-down approaches, has been the primary focus of trauma treatment, highlighting the traumatic event's logic content, and language. According to Siegel (2006), somatic and self-regulatory aspects have played a secondary role, deserting the often-nonverbal processing required to integrate and find a trauma resolution. This higher-level processing (top-down) therapies may not be enough to assist clients in the autonomic nervous system (ANS) reactions of the lower levels (bottom levels) of the brain that need acknowledgment and reprogramming for trauma healing to take place (Ogden, Pain, & Fisher, 2006).

The body has been declared to "keep the score" (Van der Kolk, 2015) or "bear the burden" (Scaer, 2014) of traumatic events. Therefore, the trauma-treating community progressively acknowledges the importance of a more embodied approach. Some trauma interventions related to somatic or physiological aspects are Somatic Experiencing, Sensorimotor Psychotherapy, EMDR, and EFT, with fluctuating levels of evidence-based or peer-reviewed research to validate effective trauma healing (Curran, 2010). Somatic interventions embrace the feelings, impulses, and movements of the body to widen the nonverbal world of the individual, steering the person to mindful awareness and increased readiness for more traditional approaches (Ogden, Minton, & Pain, 2006).

Even though EFT and EMDR are considered "bottom-up" approaches, these techniques do not eliminate the "top-down" portions of the brain or higher-level processing parts. EFT is a brief and novel intervention combining cognitive and somatic elements, significantly reducing distress by applying components of exposure, cognitive therapy, and somatic stimulation of acupressure points on the face and body (Bach et al., 2019). EFT has shown promising results in pain reduction. On a six-week EFT treatment program for chronic pain, a significant number of participants who initially met the diagnosis of Somatic Symptom Disorder, Depression, Anxiety, and Panic Disorder did not meet this after the EFT intervention. Additionally, a significant improvement occurred after the EFT treatment for all participants' quality of life and a substantial reduction in pain severity occurred after EFT treatment for all participants (Stapleton, 2022). Additionally, a study with veterans found significant drops in physical pain after EFT (Church, 2014), and when PTSD was remediated, symptoms of traumatic brain injury (TBI) reduced by 41% after three sessions (Church & Palmer-Hoffman, 2014).

Another comprehensive intervention that combines top-down and bottom-up elements is EMDR. EMDR is an empirically validated treatment for PTSD (Chambless et al., 1996; Foa et al., 2010; Shapiro, 1989). Due to its efficacy with PTSD and the high comorbidity between PTSD and chronic pain, EMDR is indicated as suitable for treating chronic pain (Roy-Byrne et al., 2004). Research shows many similarities between PTSD and chronic pain, including increased emotional liability, hyperarousal, elevated emotional distress, avoidance, and hypervigilance (Asmundsen et al., 2002; Liedl & Knaevelsrud, 2008). According to Kamińska et al. (2020), bilateral stimulation (BLS) is a crucial element of the therapeutic process in EMDR. EMDR uses BLS (eye movements, tones, taps, and vibrations, among others) to access unprocessed memories. It allows the individual to sort out these memories so they become less vivid, disturbing, or traumatic.

Another intervention that could be considered a combination of top-down and bottom-up processing is Wholistic Hybrid derived from EFT and EMDR (WHEE), which uses the right and left interhemispheric alternating of EMDR with the body focusing and positive statements of EFT (Benor et al., 2009).

Mindful breathing is another proposed mechanism for reducing stress levels and hyperarousal (Zhu et al., 2017). Mindful breathing mediates a relaxation state facilitated by parasympathetic vagus nerve stimulation by creating awareness of breathing sensations while accepting stressors such as negative emotions, upsetting thoughts, and pain (Harrison et al., 2017).

According to Schwartz and Maiberger (2018), effective trauma treatment requires a holistic methodology to help individuals cope successfully with trauma's emotional, cognitive, and somatic symptoms. This article aims to find the most efficient and integrative approach to relieving chronic pain by blending EFT's energy dimension, the interhemispheric BLS used in EMDR, the inner body-pain dialogue of WHEE, and the Quick Coherence Technique by HeartMath as a mindful breathing tool.

EFT

EFT is a simple-to-apply Energy Psychology intervention that combines exposure, cognitive therapy elements, and somatic stimulation of acupressure points on the face and body (Bach et al., 2019). It is an evidence-based practice for anxiety, depression, phobias, and PTSD when evaluated against the guidelines of the American Psychological Association's Division 12 Task Force on Empirically Validated Treatments (Church, 2013; Feinstein, 2012). EFT's efficacy in such a wide range of conditions is typically attributed to the technique's ability to reduce stress, a component of many emotional and physical disorders (Church, 2013; Lane, 2009).

Findings suggest that EFT relieves pain severity immediately while increasing individuals' capability to accept their pain (Ortner et al., 2014). Mollon (2007) describes a general decrease of client distress while tapping on acupoints and recommends this treatment as valuable for most anxiety or trauma disorders. EFT has shown notable results with pain by treating evoked pain, which influences chronic pain, and EFT has been deemed highly safe (Brattberg, 2008). A study by Flint et al. (2005) notes the lack of abreactions during Energy Psychology interventions. In a review of clinical trials, over one thousand subjects participated in EFT studies without a single adverse event, indicating a high degree of safety (Church, 2013). Individuals with pain and psychiatric disorders commonly share the physiological trait of a dysregulated ANS, particularly concerning the parasympathetic stress recovery processes (Odgen, Pain, & Fisher, 2006).

EFT has become a manualized method (Craig & Fowlie, 1995), steering the intervention toward standardized training, clinical practice, and research. EFT's effectiveness has extended across diverse populations such as veterans, chemotherapy patients, people living with a phobia, pain patients, and overweight individuals (Bach et al., 2019). Additionally, meta-analyses and systematic reviews have shown its effectiveness for physiological and psychological symptoms (Church, 2013; Feinstein, 2012).

BLS

Fundamental to the bilateral stimulation technique is the work of Francine Shapiro (2001, 2002), who developed EMDR with dual attention stimulation. Dual attention stimulation in EMDR facilitates the individual's bilateral eye movements across a focal plane. BLS was expanded to include bilateral tactile taps and auditory sounds (Tripp, 2007). Shapiro (1994) recognized bilateral tapping as equally effective as eye movements. As a result, Shapiro incorporated the BLS alternatives as valid techniques for EMDR. Shapiro (2001) suggested that past memory networks are stimulated while attention is centered on the present with external visual, auditory, or tactile cues. Shapiro also found that the brain processes traumatic memories at an accelerated rate when paired with BLS. Some research (Stickgold, 2002) suggests that the BLS used in EMDR might create interhemispheric activation in the brain, just as REM sleep does. During REM sleep, the eyes move back and forth, processing and integrating information (Parnell, 2008). When clients activate the emotions, body sensations, and thoughts associated with a disturbing memory and then add BLS, a free-association process (connection of unconscious thoughts, ideas, and beliefs) between mind and body begins (Shapiro & Maxfield, 2003).

WHEE

One intervention used in the protocol blends aspects of the widely researched interventions EMDR and EFT. WHEE is the acronym for Wholistic Hybrid derived from EMDR and EFT. Some research demonstrates its efficacy (Baisley, 2010; Benor, 2005; Benor et al., 2009, 2014, 2017). The WHEE technique involves bilateral stimulation by tapping on the right and left sides of the body while directing the thought process to the negative emotions of the traumatic event. Concurrently, the person recites affirmations to neutralize the emotional intensity of the problem at hand using EFT's Setup Statement, a sentence identifying the problem and asserting acceptance. Replacement positive statements are installed with BLS, similar to the *installation phase* in EMDR when the emotional disturbance decreases (Benor, 2008).

According to Benor (2014), the wholistic element of WHEE includes unblocking early childhood memories associated with the current problem or negative emotion being processed and addressing problematic family relationships. The author enhances the intervention with a dialogue with the body symptoms, similar to the two-chair dialogue in Gestalt therapy, while fostering intuitive awareness and accessing resources and spiritual connection. The limitation of WHEE is that it is an intervention used mainly for self-help; therefore, for the sake of simplicity, it does not include tapping on the energy meridians as in EFT.

MB

Research has demonstrated the effectiveness of mindfulness-based practices in decreasing symptoms of anxiety, depression, and chronic pain (Chiesa & Serretti, 2011; Hofmann et al., 2010). Mindful breathing (MB) is fundamental to mindfulness interventions and emphasizes nonjudgmental attention to individuals' emotional, cognitive, and physical sensations. The intervention emphasizes the experience of breathing to promote emotional and mental regulation and increasingly calmer states (Kabat-Zinn, 2003). Several studies have shown that mindful breathing can improve vagal activation through state relaxation effects (Harrison et al., 2017). Following stress, even a brief mindfulness intervention can significantly increase heart rate variability (HRV; Azam et al., 2015, 2016). The HeartMath Institute researchers introduced their innovative research on the vital role of the heart's rhythmic activity as the most sensitive measure of changes in emotional states (McCraty et al., 2009).

Additionally, HRV is produced mainly by communication between the heart and brain via neural signals flowing through ascending and descending pathways of the sympathetic and vagal branches of the ANS (Edwards, 2015). Research revealed that while positive emotions produced coherent heart rhythm marks, negative emotions were linked to irregular, incoherent heart rhythm patterns (McCraty et al., 1993). As a result, achieving heart-brain coherence through mindful breathing is a critical concept in HeartMath research. Breathing in a calm, deep, and conscious way can help mediate the human stress response, complementing the treatment of trauma and chronic pain (Lopez & Snyder, 2009).

Blending EFT, BLS, WHEE, and MB for Treating Trauma and Chronic Pain

The author of this article is a trauma counselor in private practice trained in advanced EFT and EMDR techniques. The research and information in interventions presented in this paper were part of the fulfillment of the requirements for the degree of Doctor in Social Work. The methodology, case study, and discussion herein are first-hand, based on patient interventions, combined with a current literature review of efficacy and outcome of blended interventions for trauma and chronic pain.

Efforts to blend interventions in the treatment of individuals suffering from the comorbidity of trauma and chronic pain have not been prolific, even though research suggests that integrated treatments seem to be a better alternative than parallel interventions (Otis et al., 2009).

Hartung and Galvin (2003) suggest that EMDR and Energy Psychology approaches such as EFT blend very well, each enhancing the effectiveness of the other, likening their interaction to a car's accelerating and braking controls. One of the main qualities of BLS in EMDR is to uncover hidden issues that need processing before the initial target resolves (Hartung & Galvin, 2003). As such, BLS used in EMDR will hasten the availability of emotional material and uncover memories or negative beliefs associated with the traumatic pain, bringing more knowledge related to the target of which the client is often unaware consciously (Nicosia et al., 2019).

According to Phil Mollon (2023), many practitioners of EMDR are interested in combining BLS with Energy Psychology modalities. These two interventions can create an effective and graceful synergy. The author sees eye movements or BLS as helping to evoke and deepen the thought and emotional field, while tapping the energy system then clears the associated perturbations. Although EMDR aims to help clients withstand some level of disturbance to process trauma, too much emotional upheaval can be counterproductive; therefore, blending EMDR with tapping on acupoints can decrease the emotional intensity. The practitioner can merge the two to enhance and adjust the emotional intensity of the work (Hartung & Galvin, 2003).

Traditional psychotherapy focuses on thoughts and emotions. EMDR and other interventions also do this; however, these other interventions also target the physiological body level. Energy Psychology modalities such as EFT additionally use the energy system (Mollon, n.d.). The concept of energy in Energy Psychology includes well-known principles of electrical signals, brain waves, and electromagnetic fields. These concepts have been used in describing the rapid and durable results seen in a range of health conditions after Energy Psychology interventions (Feinstein, 2022). Energy Psychology is based on the concept that traumatic experiences generate disturbances in the thought field, changes in energy flow, and vibrations in the cells, molecules, and atoms. Working with energy systems targets a more extensive range of levels than are accessed in conventional therapies (Mollon, n.d.).

The concept of human consciousness shaped as inner dialogue dates to early philosophers and intellectuals in Greece and other cultures that studied the art of communication (Billig, 1998). Many literature writers have used the landscape of inner conversations as a portal into people's unconscious (Paré & Lysack, 2006). Internal dialogues may evolve into encounters with people from the past, and, in an era in which there are high levels of cultural emphasis on mind-body approaches to healing, an "internal" dialogue between the individual and various body parts, pain, or diseases is worth exploring (Kellogg, 2004).

According to Baisley and colleague (2010), dialoguing with our pain in a WHEE session releases part of the pain effectively. In an inner dialogue in a WHEE session, we ask the pain what it is trying to tell us. This dialogue can bring about the origins of the pain, the feelings associated with it, and sometimes what we need to do or not do to heal. This internal dialogue can be applied at the start of a WHEE session and as the session progresses to address the different issues that continue arising. The body's pain appears receptive to informing from where the problem derives and "knowing" how the individual has been affected (Benor, 2008).

Mindful breathing practices have positively correlated with decreasing reactivity, the capacity to see thoughts and emotions as transitory, and withstanding adverse experiences without engaging in strict avoidance (Segal et., 2018).

An example of mindful breathing practice is the Quick Coherence Technique (HeartMath, n.d.). This breathing exercise helps individuals attain a sense of balance, coherence, and rhythm through heart-focused breathing and is considered a pivotal addition to complement "top-down" approaches with "bottom-up" processes to further achieve physiological self-regulation (Edwards, 2015).

Benor (2008) indicates that showing compassion and appreciation for the body that carries the pain could be very healing for individuals since many clients perceive the body and pain as the enemy. As a result, a modification of step two of the Quick Coherence Technique to elucidate a feeling of gratitude or appreciation for the body that carries the pain seems to be a good fit for individuals suffering from chronic pain. Adding the HeartMath Quick Coherence Technique as a mindful breathing method seems a favorable alternative to complement EFT, WHEE, and BLS.

Maximizing the practical utility of EFT, BLS, WHEE, and mindful breathing interventions using what Lazarus (1989) called "technical eclecticism" will better serve this population. Hartung and Galvin (2003) recommended that blended methodologies are suggested due to the typical complexity of pain when physical pain is partially or fully the result of psychological factors.

Suggested Protocol for Blended Interventions

The intervention proposed in this article involves the following elements: tapping the eight meridian points indicated in the EFT Basic Recipe (Church, 2018), simultaneously using a Neurotek pulser to generate the BLS used in EMDR, after eliciting a "dialogue with the body symptoms" extracted from the WHEE method and EFT. At the end of each session, the therapist assists the client with a mindful breathing intervention using the HeartMath Quick Coherence Technique showing appreciation to the body. The steps of the protocol are as follows:

1. The protocol uses two approaches to elicit the conscious and unconscious material of the pain to be processed. First, Church (2018) emphasizes the importance of being "very specific" when targeting a problem with EFT. When dealing with pain, the author suggests that the clinician should guide the client in being particular in finding pertinent information. For instance, regarding the location of the pain, an example would be "pain in the lower back on the left side," as opposed to just "pain in my back." Also, how is the person experiencing the pain, for example, "Is it a sharp, tingling, dull, throbbing, or burning pain?" To add more dimensions to the individual's experience, the clinician asks the client to describe whether the pain has a shape, color, temperature, and texture.

   The second approach to obtaining the feelings, beliefs, memories, meanings, and emotions associated with the pain is engaging in a dialog with the pain used in the WHEE method. According to Benor (2008), asking the individual, "What do you think your pain might be saying to you?" has been a key element in the success of this technique. Benor believes that even pain from surgery or an injury could carry "old" pains from earlier experiences stored in the unconscious mind. Since the human body is always striving toward health, the unconscious mind welcomes the release of these older physical and emotional pains seen through the adult's perspective, intelligence, and experiences.

   Additionally, if the pain does not relent after several rounds or sessions of processing, dialogue with the pain, asking questions such as: "Are there any reasons to hold on to this pain?" or "Is the pain ready to be released completely?" or "Are there any reasons not to reveal the reasons for this pain?" It could be beneficial to unearth buried traumatic events or secondary gains. Secondary gains are unconscious benefits that the person "enjoys" by maintaining the pain, such as financial compensation following an accident, more attention from family members, or avoidance of certain activities, thoughts, or memories. The presence of secondary gain can be a reason why an intervention may not be effective (Davidhizar, 1994; Fishbain et al., 1995).
2. The BLS used in EMDR is administered via a Neurotek pulser, a small device with two pulsars connected to a control box that vibrates episodically. A pulsar is placed in the center of each individual's palms and held securely with the thumb,

ring, and pinky finger, leaving the index and middle finger to do the EFT tapping. The pulsars can also be placed under the thighs or knees of the individual in case the person wants their hands free for EFT. If a Neurotek pulser is unavailable, clients can alternate tapping the floor with their feet while tapping the eight meridian points.

3. The subjective units of distress (SUD) scale has clients rate their level of pain and emotional disturbance using a 0–10 measure, with 0 being no distress and 10 being the worst stress imaginable. If the person feels their pain has a different rating than their emotional state, two different scales can be used.
4. Once the conscious and unconscious material regarding the pain is elucidated, and the BLS choice is established, the EFT basic recipe is performed:

   Setup Statement: "*Even though I have...* this pain that feels like... and reminds me of...and gets worse when...*I deeply and completely love and accept myself and my pain.*"

   Tap continuously on the side of the hand (SH) point while repeating the Setup Statement three times.

   While repeating the Reminder Phrase (*this pain that feels like...and reminds me of...and gets worse when...*), tap about seven times on the other seven points for three rounds: between the eyebrows (EB), on the outside edge of the eye socket (SE), underneath the eye (UE), under the nose (UN), between the lower lip and the chin (Ch), under the collarbone (CB), and about four inches below the armpit (UA).

   Test the results with a second SUD rating and ask the person for any new associations, thoughts, images, memories, emotions, feelings, or meanings after each round.
5. Close the session with the Quick Coherence Technique: "Place one hand on your heart and the other on your forehead and close your eyes."

   Step 1: "Focus your attention on the area of the heart. Imagine your breath is flowing in and out of your heart or chest area, breathing a little slower and deeper than usual. Find an easy rhythm that is comfortable for you."

   Step 2: "As you continue heart-focused breathing, make a sincere attempt to experience a regenerative feeling of appreciation and gratitude for your body that has endured this pain with you all this time."
6. Check SUD levels and associations or thoughts one last time to see if there is an additional reduction in disturbance or if there is new material to process in the next session.

The Case of Frank

The following is a case example from clinical practice describing how the protocol applied to a 45-year-old male client named Frank who had suffered from obesity and intermittent chronic back pain for over 35 years. A comprehensive intake history was taken, and rapport was easily built after two sessions. Frank verbalized that a medical condition for his pain had been ruled out and medications would only work temporarily and partially. His doctor advised Frank to explore possible psychosomatic reasons for his pain. Frank also expressed that he had insomnia, constantly felt stressed and anxious, and there were days when it was difficult getting out of bed. Psychoeducation regarding pain and its different origins and the nature of the intervention was performed. The client consented and was happy to try something different.

Frank was asked to be very specific about his pain. He stated that his pain was getting worse and was sharp on the right side of his lower back, and it felt like a cold, rugged gray rock. In answer to the question "What do you think your pain might be saying to you?" Frank, in dialoguing with the pain, disclosed that some stresses in his life from an authoritarian boss and an overbearing wife that never seemed pleased made his pain worse and made him feel resentful and helpless. Frank rated his SUD level at 8–9 at that moment. He used the Neurotek pulser in his hands, leaving the index and middle fingers for tapping. The client, with the help of the therapist, came up with this initial setup statement:

Even though I have this sharp horrible pain on the right side of my back, and it feels like a cold, gray rugged rock, and it gets worse when my boss and wife are critical, and I get resentful and helpless, I deeply and completely love and accept myself and my pain.

The client tapped three times on the side of the hand (SH) point and then three rounds on the seven additional meridian points. After this set of EFT with BLS was over, his SUD level was 6–7. When asked again to converse with his pain and body and to express any new associations, Frank got teary and said that his demanding and judgmental father came to mind. He recounted some stories about being criticized and humiliated by his father, who made him feel like he was not good enough.

Even though I still have this sharp pain on the right side of my back, and it feels like a cold, gray rugged rock, and makes me feel very sad because my father was critical and made me feel like I am not good enough, I deeply and completely love and accept myself and my pain.

After this round, Frank's SUD rating remained at 6; therefore, the clinician asked him to dialogue with his pain and if there were any reasons to hold on to it. Frank looked down and, after a while, said, "Because I am disgusting and I do not deserve to heal." After another round of EFT and BLS with the new information, his SUD level only went down to 5. The therapist asked, "Are there any reasons not to reveal the reasons for this pain?" Frank said yes reluctantly. Coming from a Hispanic family, he was raised to believe that anything that happened at home had to stay there, and even though he knew it was unfair, he felt he was disloyal to his family.

The therapist closed this session using the mindful breathing Quick Coherence Technique, which helped Frank be compassionate toward his body for the first time in his life. He verbalized that he had never liked his body and always felt like his body was not a part of him. His SUD score at the end of the session was 4. He reported feeling calm, with less pain, and a sense of relief.

In subsequent sessions using this blended protocol, Frank revealed that he had been sexually abused and sodomized for several years by his uncle, who was seven years older when Frank was only nine. At one point, he told his mother. She dismissed him by saying that had most likely not happened and never to tell that to anybody because God would punish him.

Many negative beliefs and memories were processed using the blended intervention, such as "I am disgusting," "I do not deserve to heal," "my feelings are not important," "I am unlovable," and "everything was my fault." Frank's pain sometimes increased and moved around his body through this process, but overall, he currently lives his life pain-free. He realizes now that he has a voice and that the abuse was not his fault. He has learned to take better care of himself and his body and is more compassionate toward himself. He recently changed jobs and is starting to question his marriage.

The case of Frank is fairly typical with this type of intervention in that a client coming to a session with a physical complaint, accompanied by some psychiatric symptoms such as anxiety and depression, often uncovers traumatic events holding the pain. As in the case of Frank, the process can stall, and the pain or the emotional disturbance does not move. In cases like this, the therapist needs to guide clients to deepen their inner conversation with more direct questions on why the pain remains in place or is "dangerous" to disclose. In Frank's case, his mother threatened him with "celestial punishment" if this secret was revealed, a compelling reason to maintain the status quo and not unveil the original cause of his pain.

Combining the benefits of mindful breathing and EFT as the more gentle, non-retraumatizing, and distress-reducing technique with the recovery of repressed memories through BLS and the inner-body dialogue of WHEE could prove to be an effective treatment approach for traumatized individuals with chronic pain.

Discussion

Trauma and chronic pain treatment have a wealth of research on an individual basis; however, considering the comorbidity of these ailments, their shared vulnerability, and mutual maintenance, the blending of interventions appears to be the best fit to serve traumatized individuals with chronic pain. EFT, EMDR, WHEE, and mindful breathing come from different theoretical backgrounds, have distinct procedural frameworks, and are taught as individual systems. Clinicians could integrate them to provide a rich therapeutic experience for clients and practitioners treating trauma and its damaging consequences, such as chronic pain. This article used the strengths of these methods through a sample protocol to show the potential of integrating these four effective methodologies.

Practitioners should be trained in all modalities and use their better judgment in the appropriate intervention at the right moment. The client's choice is another important consideration. Some individuals respond better or feel more comfortable with one of the interventions; therefore, clinicians should also pay attention to this critical variable. The blended protocol illustrated in this article describes a sequence of EFT, BLS, WHEE, and mindful breathing; however, considering the complexity and variations in how individuals evolve through treatment, practitioners can adapt the protocol to match clients' specific needs.

Additionally, this blended protocol could also provide a way to introduce and motivate practitioners of one of these methods to study the healing power inherent in the other methodologies. Innovative psychotherapists know that techniques such as EFT, EMDR, WHEE, and mindful breathing can provide powerful healing tools for psychological trauma but struggle to integrate them. As a result, given the prevalence of trauma and chronic pain and the lack of integrative interventions, it is essential to develop additional scholarly inquiry in treating these multiple complex issues.

Continued attention to integrative approaches to pain relief in individuals that have endured trauma will undoubtedly result in enhancements to multidisciplinary treatment and the development of efficacious coping strategies for traumatized chronic pain patients. Taking into consideration the extensive limitations in existing resources in mental health care, there is a great need for more accessible ways to disseminate evidence-based blended interventions using the technological advances that have emerged in recent years such as artificial intelligence and self-administered treatments delivered through smartphone apps or web-based platforms. Future and continuing ongoing studies are needed to continue to focus on refining the evidence of efficacy in such methods, establishing criteria for clinically significant results, and clarifying mechanisms of action.

References

Asmundson, G. J., Coons, M. J., Taylor, S., & Katz, J. (2002). PTSD and the experience of pain: Research and clinical implications of shared vulnerability and mutual maintenance models. *Canadian Journal of Psychiatry*, *47*(10), 930–937.

Asmundson, G. J., & Katz, J. (2009). Understanding the co-occurrence of anxiety disorders and chronic pain: State-of-the-art. *Depression and Anxiety*, *26*(10), 888–901.

Asmundson, G. J., Wright, K. D., & Stein, M. B. (2004). Pain and PTSD symptoms in female veterans. *European Journal of Pain*, *8*(4), 345–350.

Azam, M. A., Katz, J., Fashler, S. R., Changoor, T., Azargive, S., & Ritvo, P. (2015). Heart rate variability is enhanced in controls but not maladaptive perfectionists during brief mindfulness meditation following stress-induction: A stratified-randomized trial. *International Journal of Psychophysiology*, *98*(1), 27–34.

Azam, M. A., Katz, J., Mohabir, V., & Ritvo, P. (2016). Individuals with tension and migraine headaches exhibit increased heart rate variability during post-stress mindfulness meditation practice but a decrease during a post-stress control condition–A randomized, controlled experiment. *International Journal of Psychophysiology*, *110*, 66–74.

Bach, D., Groesbeck, G., Stapleton, P., Sims, R., Blickheuser, K., & Church, D. (2019). Clinical EFT (Emotional Freedom Techniques) improves multiple physiological markers of health. *Journal of Evidence-Based Integrative Medicine*, *24*, 2515690X18823691.

Baisley, A., & Ed, M. A. (2010). The benefits and potentials of WHEE: Wholistic Hybrid derived from EMDR and EFT. *International Journal of Healing and Caring, 10*(2).

Beckham, J. C., Crawford, A. L., Feldman, M. E., Kirby, A. C., Hertzberg, M. A., Davidson, J. R. T., & Moore, S. D. (1997). Chronic posttraumatic stress disorder and chronic pain in Vietnam combat veterans. *Journal of Psychosomatic Research*, *43*(4), 379–389.

Benor, D. J. (2005). Self-healing interventions for clinical practice: Brief psychotherapy with WHEE—the wholistic hybrid of EMDR and EFT. *Complementary Therapies in Clinical Practice*, *11*(4), 270–274.

Benor, D. J. (2008). *Seven minutes to natural pain release: WHEE for tapping your pain away—The revolutionary new self-healing method.* Energy Psychology Press.

Benor, D. J. (2014). Energy psychology: Practices and theories of new combinations of psychotherapy. *Current Research in Psychology*, *5*(1), 1–18.

Benor, D. J., Ledger, K., Toussaint, L., Hett, G., & Zaccaro, D. (2009). Pilot study of EFT, WHEE and CBT for treatment of test anxiety in university students. *Explore: The Journal of Science and Healing*, *5*(6), 338–340.

Benor, D., Rossiter-Thornton, J., & Toussaint, L. (2017). A randomized, controlled trial of wholistic hybrid derived from eye movement desensitization and reprocessing and emotional freedom technique (WHEE) for self-treatment of pain, depression, and anxiety in chronic pain patients. *Journal of Evidence-Based Complementary and Alternative Medicine*, *22*(2), 268–277.

Billig, M. (1998). Rhetoric and the unconscious. *Argumentation*, *12*(2), 199–216.

Brattberg, G. (2008). Self-administered EFT (Emotional Freedom Techniques) in individuals with fibromyalgia: A randomized trial. *Integrative Medicine*, *7*(4), 30–35.

Chambless, D. L., Sanderson, W. C., Shoham, V., Johnson, S. B., Pope, K. S., Crits-Christoph, P., … McCurry, S. (1996). An update on empirically validated therapies. *Clinical Psychologist*, *49*(2), 5–18.

Chiesa, A., & Serretti, A. (2011). Mindfulness-based interventions for chronic pain: A systematic review of the evidence. *Journal of Alternative and Complementary Medicine*, *17*(1), 83–93.

Church, D. (2013). Clinical EFT as an evidence-based practice for the treatment of psychological and physiological conditions. *Psychology*, *4*(8), 645–654.

CLINICAL REPORT

Single-Session Reductions in Emotional Distress in an Addiction Clinic after Thought Field Therapy Treatment

Jennifer Cribbs, Pittsburgh, Pennsylvania, USA

Abstract

Thought Field Therapy (TFT) is a promising psychotherapy approach due to its ability to relieve human suffering rapidly. This brief intervention is an energy-based therapy that is proving to be an effective treatment for a wide range of clinical conditions. Numerous studies have shown that the use of tapping can produce immediate, long-lasting results. Drawing from information gathered at SpiritLife, an inpatient drug and alcohol rehabilitation facility, this research examined the effects of a single TFT session on individuals who have been diagnosed with a substance use disorder and have been experiencing distress related to trauma. Thirty-seven participants (17 male and 20 female), aged 23–37, used the Subjective Units of Distress (SUD) scale to rate their symptoms prior to and after a single session. A statistically significant decrease in symptoms was observed in 100% of participants postintervention ($p < .00$). This further supports other clinical trials indicating that TFT is an effective treatment for a variety of psychological conditions and emotional distress. While Energy Psychology can be applied as an independent therapeutic modality, the mechanisms of the intervention allow practitioners to integrate it easily into an existing clinical framework.

Keywords: Thought Field Therapy, TFT, addiction, trauma, emotional distress, energy psychology, tapping, energy-based, Callahan, holistic, meridian points

Jennifer Cribbs, LSW, is a licensed social worker providing therapeutic services to highly motivated individuals at Choices Clinical Counseling, a family owned and operated counseling center. **Correspondence:** Jennifer Cribbs, University of Pittsburgh, School of Social Work, 4200 Fifth Avenue, Pittsburgh, PA 15260; email: jennycribbs98@yahoo.com. **Disclosure:** The author declares no conflict of interest.

Individuals who have experienced trauma from childhood onward make up the majority of clients served in the mental health and substance abuse systems (Rosenberg, 2011). The greater the trauma, the greater the risk for substance abuse, alcoholism, and other negative outcomes. Trauma is described as an individual's response to witnessing or experiencing a frightening event, such as sexual assault, military combat, or a life-threatening accident. Studies suggest that initial reactions to trauma can include exhaustion, confusion, sadness, anxiety, dissociation, and/or physical arousal (Bray, 2006).

Trauma is a risk factor for nearly all substance use disorders. Often, experiencing a traumatic event leads directly to substance use as a method to cope with the undesirable memories and emotions related to the event. According to the self-medication hypothesis, people attempt to manage or counteract their distressing symptoms by using substances or alcohol to numb themselves of the negative feelings (NCTSN, 2008). The National Vietnam Readjustment Study was conducted in the 1980s. It found that 74% of Vietnam Veterans who were diagnosed with posttraumatic stress disorder (PTSD) also had a co-occurring substance use disorder (Galindo, 2020). Practitioners are essential in providing interventions that can help empower these individuals to improve their quality of life after experiencing a traumatic event.

Thought Field Therapy (TFT)

TFT is proving to be an innovative and effect psychotherapy tool that can be used to treat trauma, anxiety, PTSD, substance abuse, stress, and many other disorders (Connolly, 2022). This has been demonstrated by quickly and dramatically eliminating distressing symptoms for a substantial number of people (Mollon, 2007). It is hypothesized that when tapping on certain points on the body (see Appendix A), electrochemical impulses are sent to the areas of the brain that regulate the fear and stress response (Mollon, 2007).

As American psychologist Roger Callahan developed TFT in the 1980s, he found that emotions are correlated with various diseases, which are consequences of inadequate flow of the vital force that circulates through precise points in the body (Barraza-Alvarez, 2021). Tapping can restore that flow. An important event happened for Callahan when he was treating a patient named Mary in 1979. Mary had a long-standing fear of water (aquaphobia) and Callahan was making little progress using traditional methods, such as cognitive and behavioral methods (Mollon, 2007). When Callahan was attempting exposure therapy with Mary, Mary still felt uneasy, specifically in her stomach. Callahan discovered that after Mary tapped on her stomach meridian, she felt instant relief and she declared her fear was gone in a matter of moments.

TFT has been gaining traction over the years; it's an appealing approach in that it is quick, non-invasive, and economical. Moreover, it can be used in conjunction with other modalities to complement any traditional treatment being provided. TFT has been determined to be a safe, effective, and a culturally adaptable approach (Sakai et al., 2001).

Psychological Mechanisms of TFT

Research has evidenced promising results with TFT for children exposed to trauma. The dire psychological and physiological consequences of childhood trauma have been extensively reviewed and reported (Sakai et al., 2010). A 2006 study in Rwanda investigated the outcomes of TFT for children who had survived genocide and been diagnosed with PTSD. The children's PTSD symptoms were significantly reduced immediately following the treatment sessions as well as at the one-year follow up session (Sakai et al., 2010).

An article written by David Feinstein (2021) analyzed a database of peer-reviewed journal articles that explored the effects of Energy Psychology (EP). Energy Psychology is an umbrella term for treatment approaches that incorporate an energetic component, including a focus on the body's well-established electromagnetic activity and subtle energies described in ancient healing traditions such as the flow of energy through acupuncture meridians (Feinstein, 2021). One of the most popular variations of Energy Psychology is TFT. This method combines the stimulation of electrochemically sensitive points on the skin (by tapping or holding them) while either imagining the past trauma or thinking about the stressor (Feinstein, 2021). The points used in these protocols are the same points used in acupuncture. Feinstein's review found empirically supported evidence to suggest the efficacy of Energy Psychology in reducing symptoms associated with trauma.

According to a large South American study, tapping was substantially superior to conventional methods such as cognitive behavioral therapy (CBT; Mollon, 2007). In this study, researchers examined about 29,000 patients with mental health problems over a 14-year period and found the results to be striking. Simple, rhythmic tapping proved a remarkable form of desensitization that brought instant relief for patients. Later, a subgroup of 5,000 patients were examined more closely. Of the patients who received CBT, 63% reported relief of distressing symptoms, while 90% of patients in the tapping group reported relief of distressing symptoms (Mollon, 2007). Even more promising is that 51% of the CBT group and 76% of the tapping group had complete relief of symptoms (Mollon, 2007). It was also noted that the tapping group required fewer sessions than the traditional psychotherapy.

TFT and Substance Abuse

TFT has also gained recognition in the field of substance abuse treatment. In 2016, TFT was listed for the treatment for PTSD symptoms on the National Registry of Evidence-based Programs and Practices (NREPP) of the Substance Abuse and Mental Health Services Administration (SAMHSA; McAninch, 2016) in the United States. One of the key components of this method is that there are no apparent side effects, therefore, it will not cause harm. Considering the complexity of trauma and substance use disorders, using a holistic approach is important.

Decades of research show a direct link between the exposure of a traumatic event and the development of a substance use disorder

(Galindo, 2020). Conversely, individuals with a substance use disorder are more likely to experience a traumatic event, leaving individuals in a perpetual cycle of co-occurrence. Traditionally, those who have trauma disorders with a co-occurring substance use disorder have experienced poorer outcomes because previous treatment modalities have focused on one disorder at a time (Galindo, 2020). However, the more we understand the complexities of these disorders, the more we can focus our efforts on creating a treatment that addresses the individual holistically, with a recovery mindset and an emphasis on building resiliency.

Having co-occurring disorders not only affects the accessibility to treatment, but clients with a dual diagnosis tend to have poorer outcomes. According to a study by Popescu (2021), Energy Psychology is an empowering and effective adjunct treatment for those with co-occurring disorders. This approach, combined with existing treatment paradigms, offers the tools to empower clients by rewiring and re-regulating their trauma response.

The Association for Comprehensive Energy Psychology (ACEP) maintains an up-to-date database for Energy Psychology and related topics that are listed in indexing services such as PubMed, PsychInfo, and Medline (Feinstein, 2021). According to the website, "as of February 2022, over 70 randomized controlled trials, over 55 pre-post outcome studies, 5 meta-analysis, and 19 systematic reviews have been published in English-speaking, peer-reviewed journals" (ACEP, 2022). Energy Psychology is not only evidence-based, but it is also in the top 10% of published research for psychotherapy modalities (ACEP, 2022).

Methods

The purpose of this research study is to answer the question: Is Thought Field Therapy (TFT) an effective intervention to reduce emotional distress related to experiencing trauma in clients diagnosed with a substance use disorder? This research assessed the effectiveness of the TFT intervention, an existing program within SpiritLife, by utilizing an 11-point Subjective Units of Distress (SUD) scale. Clients rated their level of distress before and after the intervention. It was hypothesized that the TFT intervention would provide immediate physical and emotional relief from distress that would, in turn, promote health and overall well-being.

SpiritLife is an inpatient, 58-bed, drug and alcohol rehabilitation and detox center in Penn Run, Pennsylvania, that offers short and long-term care (SpiritLife, 2021). The mission of SpiritLife is that "recovery is a process of change through which individuals improve their health and wellness, live self-directed lives, and strive to reach their full potential." In the course of treatment, clients are provided psycho-education on the disease of addiction, learn relapse prevention skills, and have access to evidence-based, trauma-informed care. It is the goal of the clinical staff to find a pathway of recovery that works best for each individual. Because there is not a "one size fits all" type of intervention, SpiritLife uses the strategy of exposing clients to a variety of intervention techniques, aimed at treating the whole person: mind, body, and spirit. This includes the implementation of six treatment modalities: Clinical Group Therapy, Adventure Track, Spirituality, Meditation, Musicology, and Trauma-Focused Therapy. TFT is integrated with the other six modalities at SpiritLife to address both the mental health and the substance abuse disorders in clients.

Trauma specialist Jim McAninch has been working in the field for over 20 years, implementing TFT with patients to address the co-occurrence of trauma and substance use disorder. McAninch is a Registered Certified Recovery Coach, NES Health Practitioner, and the founder of UR Energy Wellness Coaching (Ceparano, 2022). According to McAninch, many of our struggles come from programs in our subconscious minds. Most of the programs we get are self-sabotaging, disempowering, and limiting. Ninety-five percent of the time, our minds are operating from the subconscious mind (Callaghan, 2021). McAninch incorporates trauma-informed techniques to help his clients access the subconscious and look for blockages that are getting in the way of recovery. This method helps individuals release the subconscious beliefs they hold as a result of the trauma they have experienced.

Using Roger Callahan's techniques, McAninch first has the client think about their most troublesome issue. Next, the client is guided through tapping, on their own body, on the energy points, in a specific order. One of the unique benefits of this technique is that clients are able to work through their negative energy blockages without having to talk about or relive the traumatic events. McAninch implements TFT in a single session that lasts approximately one to two hours. Clients regularly report immediate relief following their session.

This study uses a pre- and posttest design to examine the effectiveness of TFT. The study examined changes in distress levels before and after one session of TFT. All participants were provided with a single session of TFT. Using the 11-point SUD scale, participants' self-reported distress levels were measured prior to and after the session. Data were gathered from 37 participants of SpiritLife from February 2022 to April 2022. Participants were drawn from a single-site inpatient drug and alcohol facility, using convenience sampling of clients who had been admitted to SpiritLife, were diagnosed with a substance use disorder, and reported a history of trauma.

The Subjective Units of Distress (SUD) scale was developed by behavioral therapist Joseph Wolpe (1969) as an instrument for measuring anxiety in exposure-based therapies (Kim et al., 2008). Further study of the validity of the SUD scale found a strong correlation between initial SUD scores and both the Beck's Depression Inventory (BDI) and State Anxiety Inventory (SAI) in participants (Kim et al., 2008). This indicated that the SUD rating is related to the patient's current level of depression and anxiety, therefore demonstrating convergent validity.

In the present study, SUD scores were used to measure the participant's level of distress prior to the intervention and following the intervention. As one of the tenets of TFT is to reduce emotional and physical distress, the SUD scale is considered a reliable instrument. The SUD scores range from 0 to 10, with the lowest being 0 (no distress/totally relaxed) and the highest being 10 (the most anxiety/distress that one has ever felt); see Appendix B.

The objective of this research was to determine if TFT is an effective treatment modality for those suffering with symptoms of trauma. Descriptive statistics were used to describe the sample used in the present study. Data were analyzed using SPSS, version 26, for descriptive statistics and paired t-test results.

Results

The findings of this study demonstrate the ratings of 37 clients at SpiritLife, a drug and alcohol treatment program, who received the TFT intervention; 17 respondents (45.9%) were male and 20 respondents (54.1%) were female. All participants were diagnosed with a substance use disorder and reported at least one traumatic event that had caused physical or emotional symptoms of stress. After the intervention, all participants reported a decrease in symptoms of distress. Table 1 shows that preintervention all 37 participants rated their SUD level between 8 and 10. After one session of TFT, all participants rated their SUD level in the range of 0 to 5.

There was a significant average difference between pretest and posttest SUD scores ($p < .00$). The 37 clients who received TFT reported a significant reduction in distress postintervention. The mean pretest SUD score was 9, meaning clients reported, on average, feeling extremely anxious/distressed prior to the intervention. Conversely, the mean posttest SUD score was 2, meaning clients reported, on average, feeling alert, awake, and very little distress immediately following the intervention.

All participants reported a decrease in their level of distress. Some participants claimed that TFT provided immediate relief from suffering they had been struggling with for years. They reported the following:

- "I originally rated my distress at a 10. I felt trauma first when I was 2 years old and that has lived within me until now. There was internal conflict that I couldn't ever get over. After my session with Jim, I felt extremely relieved and I found it very helpful."
- "My anxiety was at a 10. I had resentment from a past relationship and ongoing issues around my parents' divorce. After my session with Jim, I felt extremely relieved. I would recommend these sessions to others."
- "I'd say my distress was about a 9. I felt like I had no closure from the death of my

Table 1. *Descriptive Statistics: Pre- and Postintervention SUD Scores*

	Respondents	SUD Score (Lowest)	SUD Score (Highest)	Mean	Std. Deviation
Preintervention	37	8	10	9.38	.681
Postintervention	37	0	5	1.92	1.754

Note. 37 Respondents: 17 males, 20 females, ages 23–37.

boyfriend and I've been angry at his mother. I also have anger at my own mother for having no relationship and feeling like she never really wanted me. After the session, I felt fairly relieved. It was definitely helpful."

Discussion

One of the first steps in working with those who have experienced traumatic events is helping them manage the overwhelming feelings and symptoms of trauma. Some of the most common symptoms of trauma, similar to symptoms of a substance use disorder, include intrusive thoughts, anxiety, mood swings, nightmares, guilt or shame, feeling sad or hopeless, or loss of memory or concentration skills. TFT can end emotional and physical symptoms in a matter of moments (Bray, 2006). Another beneficial aspect of this modality is that it does not require the individual to talk about or relive the traumatic event. It is unnecessary to dredge up old memories through traditional talk therapy. According to psychotherapist Peter Levine, PhD, the developer of Somatic Experiencing and author of *Waking the Tiger: Healing Trauma,* the key to healing trauma is understanding the physiological symptoms and allowing the nervous system to dispel the body's instinctual fear response (Levine, 1997).

The purpose of this research study was to answer the question: Is Thought Field Therapy (TFT) an effective intervention to reduce emotional distress related to experiencing trauma in clients diagnosed with a substance use disorder? The results indicate that following one session of TFT, client's levels of distress decreased significantly ($p < .00$). The most significant finding is that 100% of all participants had a reduction in symptoms. This indicates that TFT serves as an effective and safe therapeutic tool to reduce negative emotions associated with past traumas and ongoing life challenges.

It appears that a single session of TFT can effectively and efficiently reduce the perceived intensity of distress and improve physiological symptoms. These findings are consistent with the multitude of clinician and client reports regarding the immediate impact of TFT. As observed at SpiritLife, clients felt relief directly after their session. By implementing TFT, along with the additional treatment modalities, SpiritLife is able to treat the individual holistically. The hope for this research, along with future studies that will follow, is that practitioners will embrace TFT as a viable modality worthy of learning and integrating into everyday practice. By working with the body's own ability to encode and release emotional information, TFT can be that missing piece that vastly enhances the effectiveness of psychotherapy.

References

Good Therapy. (2022). *Thought Field Therapy.* Retrieved from http://www.goodtherapy.org/learn-about-therapy/types/thought-field-therapy

Association for Comprehensive Energy Psychology (ACEP). (2022). *Energy psychology research.* Retrieved from https://www.energypsych.org/researchdb8c71b7

Barraza-Alvarez, F. V. (2021). Callahan's thought field therapy in the management of emotions associated with stress. *World Journal of Biology Pharmacy and Health Sciences, 7*(2), 060–068.

Bray, R. L. (2006). Thought Field Therapy: Working through traumatic stress without the overwhelming responses. *Journal of Aggression, Maltreatment and trauma, 12*(1–2), 103–123.

Callaghan, R. (2021). *Our 3 brains—Why 95% of our behaviors are not conscious.* Retrieved from http://rorycallaghan.com/our-3-brains-why-95-of-our-behaviors-are-not-conscious/amp

Ceparano, L. (2022). James McAninch of UR Energy Wellness Coaching to be featured on Close Up Radio. *EIN NewsDesk.* Retrieved from http://www.einnews.com

Connolly, S. (2022). *Thirteen evidence based Thought Field Therapy studies and nine reviews supporting TFT's effectiveness.* Retrieved from https://www.thoughtfieldtherapy.net/wp-content/uploads/2023/03/References-2023-03-13.pdf

Feinstein, D. (2021). Six empirically-supported premises about energy psychology: Mounting evidence for a controversial therapy. *Advances in Mind-Body Medicine, 35*(2), 17–32.

Feinstein, D. (2022). The energy of energy psychology. *OBM Integrative and Complementary Medicine, 7*(2), 1–28.

Galindo, N. (2020). *The connection between substance use and trauma* [Blog post]. Retrieved from http://www.relias.com/blog/connection-substance-use-and-trauma

Kim, D., Bae, H., & Chon Park, Y. (2008). Validity of the Subjective Units of Disturbance scale in EMDR. *Journal of EMDR Practice and Research, 2*(1), 57–62.

Levine, P. A. (1997). *Waking the Tiger: Healing Trauma.* North Atlantic Books.

McAninch, J. (2016). Helping the 911 dispatchers with Thought Field Therapy. *International Journal of Healing and Caring, 16*(2), 1–16.

Mollon. (2007, December 3). Thought Field Therapy and its derivatives: Rapid relief of mental health problems through tapping on the body. *Primary Care and Community Psychiatry, 12*(3/4), 123–127.

National Childhood Traumatic Stress Network (NCTSN). (2008). *Making the connection: Trauma and substance abuse.* Retrieved from https://www.nctsn.org/sites/default/files/resources/making_the_connection_trauma_substance_abuse.pdf

Popescu, A. (2021). Trauma-based energy psychology treatment is associated with client rehabilitation at an addiction clinic. *Energy Psychology: Theory, Research, and Treatment, 13*(1), 12–29.

Rosenberg, L. (2011). Addressing trauma in mental health and substance use treatment. *Journal of Behavioral Health Services and Research, 38*(4), 428–431.

Sakai, C., Paperny, D., Mathews, M., Tanida, G., Boyd, G., Simons, A., … Nutter, L. (2001). Thought Field Therapy clinical applications: Utilization in an HMO in behavioral medicine and behavioral health services. *Journal of Clinical Psychology, 57*(10), 1215–1227.

Sakai, C. E., Connolly, S. M., & Oas, P. (2010). Treatment of PTSD in Rwandan child genocide survivors using Thought Field Therapy. *International Journal of Emergency Mental Health, 12*(1), 41–50.

SpiritLife. (2021). Retrieved from http://www.spiritlifeinc.org

Wolpe, J. (1969). *The practice of behavior therapy.* Pergamon Press.

APPENDIX A

Chart of Tapping Points

THE CALLAHAN TECHNIQUES

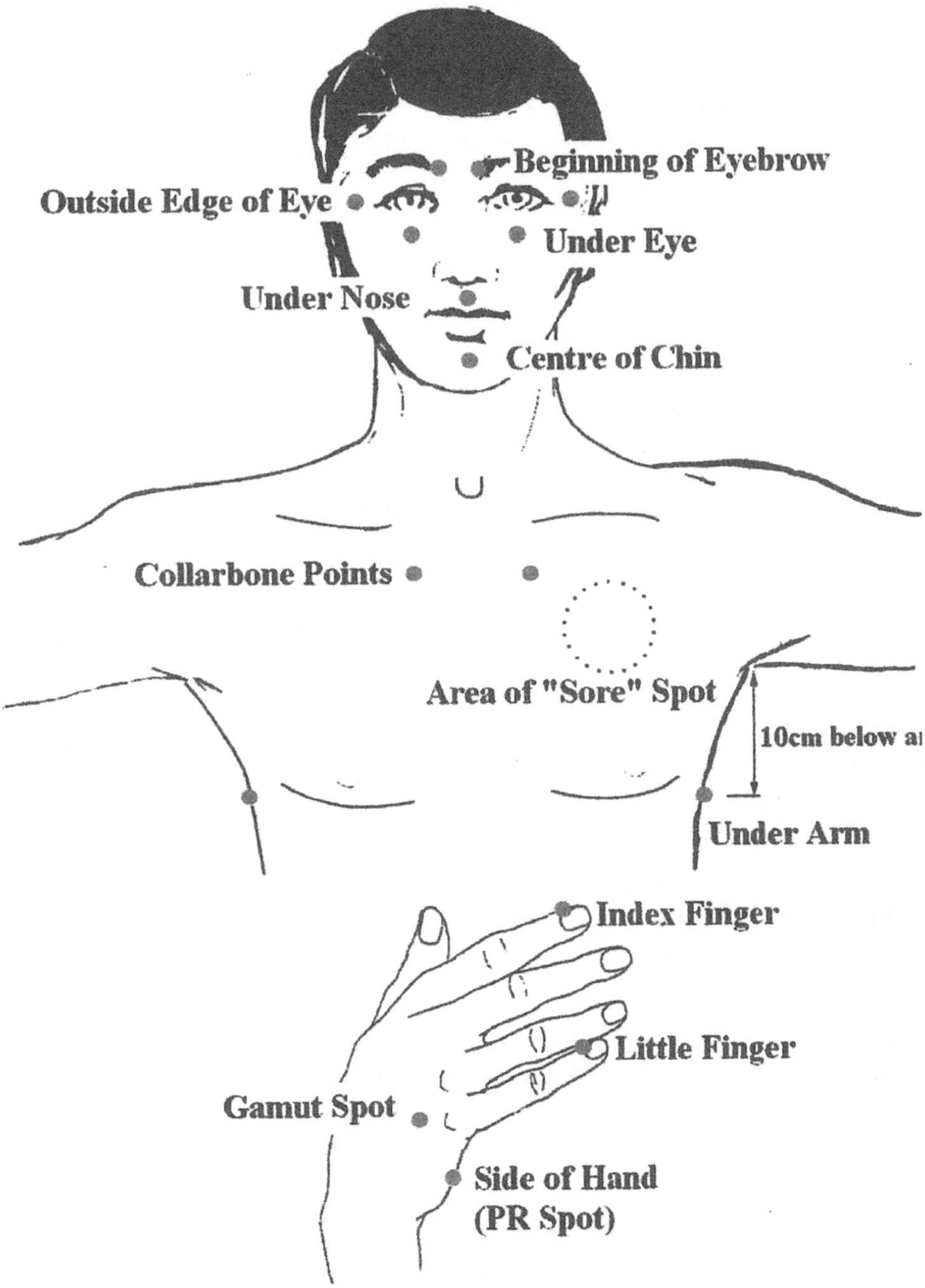

www.RogerCallahan.com

APPENDIX B

SUD Scale and Rating Form

Please indicate your initial level of Distress:

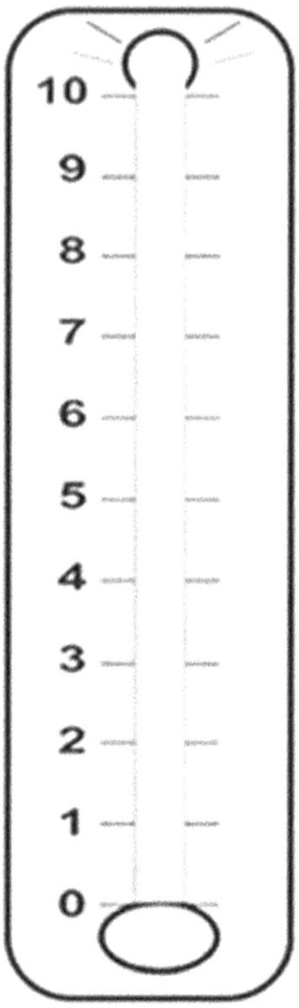

10 - Highest distress/fear/anxiety/discomfort that you have ever felt

9 - Extremely anxious/distressed

8 - Very anxious/distressed, can't concentrate

7 - Quite anxious/distressed, interfering with performance

6 -

5 - Moderate anxiety/distress, uncomfortable but can continue to perform

4 -

3 - Mild anxiety/distress, no interference with performance

2 - Minimal anxiety/distress

1 - Alert and awake, concentrating well

0 - Totally relaxed

After my session with Jim, I feel: (Please use numerical rating, based on the scale above)

- **EXTREMELY RELIEVED**
- **FAIRLY RELIEVED**
- **NO CHANGE AT ALL**

Comments:

I would/would not recommend these sessions to other clients.

I permit this confidential information to be used for research to help the work with other clients.

INTIALS:______________________________ **DATE:**__________________________

CLINICAL REPORT

Advanced Integrative Therapy: Origins, Research, Theory, and Practice

Gregory Brown, Kirk Kerkorian School of Medicine, University of Nevada Las Vegas, USA
Elizabeth V. Pace, New Orleans, Louisiana, USA
Tabatha Bird Weaver, Newberg, Oregon, USA

Abstract
Advanced Integrative Therapy (AIT) is a novel therapy grounded in Energy Psychology combined with cognitive and somatic therapy techniques. As more research is being conducted into the efficacy of AIT and other trauma-based therapies, there is a need to define the modality more clearly for researchers, the clinical community, and potential clients. This article aims to discuss the theory behind AIT and its mechanism of action, compare it with other somatic trauma and Energy Psychology techniques, and explore the gap in the available data and knowledge of AIT. Additionally, a case study will be discussed to report on the potential clinical effectiveness of AIT in treating trauma-related dissociation.

Keywords: Advanced Integrative Therapy, AIT, trauma, healing, psychology, energy psychology, cognitive somatic therapy, somatic

Gregory Brown, MD, is a professor of psychiatry at the Kirk Kerkorian School of Medicine, Department of Psychiatry and Behavioral Health, University of Nevada Las Vegas, where he is also the director of residency training, in addition to maintaining an active private practice. **Elizabeth V. Pace, LPCS**, is a mental health therapist in private practice in New Orleans, Louisiana. **Tabatha Bird Weaver, MA**, is a licensed professional counselor, licensed marriage and family therapist, and certified alcohol and drug counselor in private practice specializing in complex trauma, neurodiversity, and recovery. **Correspondence:** Gregory Brown, MD, Kirk Kerkorian School of Medicine at UNLV, Department of Psychiatry and Behavioral Health, 3014 West Charleston Blvd., Suite 130, Las Vegas, NV 89102. **Disclosure:** The authors declare no conflict of interest.

Advanced Integrative Therapy (AIT) is a trauma treatment, and it is the stance of AIT's progenitor, Asha Clinton, MSW, PhD, that trauma is the cause of most psychological disorders (Clinton, 2010). In Bessel van der Kolk's seminal work on trauma, *The Body Keeps the Score,* he notes that trauma is experienced in the body, including an overactive "threat" response; thus, a trauma treatment that does not include somatized feelings, emotions, and sensations may fail to treat trauma thoroughly and thereby bring lasting healing for those suffering from traumatic symptoms (van der Kolk, 2015).

Advanced Integrative Therapy is commonly described as an Energy Psychology (EP) intervention but can also be compared to other somatic therapies. EP is a type of therapy that combines cognitive interventions with somatic techniques that influence human bioenergy systems. It is used in many therapeutic settings, ranging from performance enhancement to severe traumatic distress. EP practitioners view symptoms as systemic, interactive bioenergetic patterns. This means that there is constant and complex communication among neurobiological processes, electrophysiology, consciousness, and bioenergy systems. These systems include stimulation of meridians, chakras, and the biofield, as well as subtler systems of the body such as neuroception. The interaction between these systems during EP interventions appears to increase the speed and/or thoroughness of treatment by interrupting electrical or chemical pathways between the locus of distress in the body and the brain. This results in normalized cortisol levels (Church et al., 2012) and balance between the sympathetic and parasympathetic nervous systems

(Bach et al., 2019), which thereby allows a thorough adaptive integration of the experience, thus reducing symptoms of depression, anxiety, and posttraumatic stress, as well as other concerns.

A systematic review and meta-analysis published in 2015 (Nelms & Castel, 2016) concluded that Energy Psychology interventions are effective for treating depression, as one example, with an average effect size of $d = 0.82$. Another article regarding agoraphobia (Irgens et al., 2017) found that Energy Psychology was as effective as or more effective than traditional psychotherapy. The most common Energy Psychology methods are Emotional Freedom Techniques (EFT), Thought Field Therapy (TFT), Tapas Acupressure Technique (TAT), and Advanced Integrative Therapy (AIT).

While cognitive behavioral and exposure-based interventions may relieve some of the psychological symptoms from past traumatic events, research has found that psychotherapy or language-based interventions require a substantial capacity for cognitive processing, which many severely traumatized clients do not possess (Kuhfuß et al., 2021). For clients whose ability for cognitive processing is compromised by increased negative affect or limbic system overactivation, talk therapy may be ineffective or even counterproductive at times, and exposure therapy may be too confrontational.

Somatic Therapies

Somatic Experiencing (SE) is described as a "body-oriented therapeutic approach that treats post-traumatic symptoms by changing the interoceptive and proprioceptive sensations associated with the traumatic experience" (Kuhfuß et al., 2021). Similarly, AIT is a gentle, body-oriented therapeutic approach that focuses on reducing the client's residual sensory distress associated with past traumatic experiences. The mindfulness of somatic disturbance and its associated sensations in the body downregulates the fight-or-flight response in the ANS and desensitizes and reprocesses traumatic memories, as it is associated with hand placement in AIT.

Preliminary Evidence and Research on AIT

Case Studies

Two case studies have been published to date that focus on the efficacy of AIT. The first case study, published in 2021 in the *International Journal of Healing and Caring*, was a retroactive case report in which the clinician utilized compassion-focused therapy, Eye Movement Desensitization and Reprocessing (EMDR), and AIT (Pace, 2021). The relative effectiveness of the treatment modalities was compared using the Subjective Units of Distress (SUD) rating associated with traumatic memories.

The client concluded that, of the three treatment modalities, AIT was what ultimately allowed her to extinguish the stored emotions attached to the trauma. The client reported that AIT allowed her to become more cognizant of her body and her emotions, which in turn helped increase her confidence and self-efficacy. She stated, "Embodiment allows me to know whether or not relationships are safe places for me to grow," and reported that AIT increased her feelings of trust in herself (Pace, 2021).

Given that this was a retroactive case study utilizing three different treatment modalities, it is useful to note the similarities in memory reconsolidation and reprocessing between AIT and EMDR sessions.

The second AIT case study, published in 2021 in *Energy Psychology,* was a hermeneutic single-case efficacy design that documented remarkable outcomes from seven sessions of AIT (Bird Weaver, 2012). The client reentered treatment for an increase of anxiety, relational distress, and fibromyalgia experienced when she accepted custody of a sibling's child. The client's progress was assessed using the PTSD Checklist for DSM-5 (PCL-5; Weathers et al., 2013) to measure posttraumatic stress disorder (PTSD) symptoms; the International Trauma Questionnaire (ITQ; Cloitre et al., 2018) to measure C-PTSD symptoms according to the criteria of the World Health Organization International Classification of Diseases, 11th revision (ICD-11; WHO, 2021); the Child-Parent Relationship Scale (CPRS; Pianta, 1992) to measure connection and conflict in the caregiver-child relationship; and the Subjective Units of Distress (SUD) scale (Wolpe, 1969) to rate the client's current level of distress or discomfort. The clinician also used the self-report questionnaire Helpful Aspects of Therapy (HAT; Llewelyn et al., 1988) and the Change Interview (CI) method (Elliott et al., 2001) to measure client experience and perspective.

The client demonstrated dramatic and global improvement after treatment with AIT. This client scored near the upper threshold on both the PCL-5 and the ITQ-11 at the start of treatment. Within three AIT sessions, the client no longer met diagnostic criteria for PTSD or C-PTSD. Additionally, the CPRS showed dramatic changes in intergenerational relationship satisfaction: the scores of conflict and connection inverted.

This study provided a brief overview of AIT theory and protocols, as well as detailed notes of the trauma content that the client processed in easy-to-follow tables. As this was an individual case study, generalizability of this type of result is unknown. However, the data in this study do imply that AIT was the primary driver of change, as the client had previously been treated numerous times with other therapy modalities with minimal progress in symptom reduction. In the client's own words, "I was headed in a direction of crashing and burning—in a significant amount of pain, always exhausted, always emotionally triggered, always feeling hopeless and overwhelmed, and just continuing to feel worse and worse. Once we started AIT, I very quickly progressed to feeling the way that I feel now. So undoubtedly, there's no question that this is what did it" (Bird Weaver, 2021).

Books

Two recent books have made particular reference to AIT-based treatment. In *Treating Trauma with Energy Psychology,* Catherine Folkers, MSW, provides a series of documented case reports in which AIT was used as a primary treatment modality for phobias, PTSD, complex trauma, borderline personality, and psychosomatic conditions (Folkers, 2022). The publication also reviews the basic concepts of AIT and elements of its application.

In *Sacred Medicine: A Doctor's Quest to Unravel the Mysteries of Healing*, Lissa Rankin, MD, describes the AIT model and case examples, in addition to providing the Quick AIT Protocol for practical self-use. Rankin is a medical doctor who has shifted into alternative medicine for growth and self-healing. She describes AIT as: "a complete energy psychotherapy with Jungian roots, aspects of Gestalt therapy, some self-psychology, and influences from Buddhism and Sufism. AIT is based on a set of protocols and other methods with a psychodynamic, cognitive-behavioral, and transpersonal theoretical treatment for trauma and its resultant mental, physical, emotional, foundation that provides thorough, deep, and relatively painless and spiritual health challenges" (Rankin, 2022, p. 277).

Therapist Response Study

A recent study (Brown et al., 2022) surveyed AIT-based therapists to assess their perspective of therapeutic response with AIT clients. Seventy-six responses were received from experienced AIT therapists, a large percentage of whom had used the modality within the past few months with active patients. In 77% of the sessions, the therapists were able to extinguish patterns of negative emotions rooted in multiple past events rather than single events. Over 75% of the events were identified as originating in childhood or being chronic in nature.

The sessions began with an average SUD score reported as 8.3 out of 10 (with 0 being no distress and 10 being the greatest distress imaginable). In 92% of cases, a single session of AIT effectively reduced the SUD score to either 0 or 1, which on average took about three rounds of AIT sessions. Any associated physical sensations, when present, were also fully extinguished in a similar percentage of individuals. The study outcome was based on the client-reported changes in SUD scores and the therapist's perception of treatment efficacy. As such, one may consider a potential positive bias on the part of the therapist respondents in regard to the study findings.

Proposed Mechanisms of Change

Energetic Systems

While there is a plethora of evidence demonstrating the efficacy of energetic interventions on both physiological and psychological systems, the specific mechanisms of change are only recently emerging with new research. Studies of acupoints identified by traditional Chinese medicine (TCM) have demonstrated chemical changes in the hypothalamic-pituitary-adrenal and endogenous opioid systems (Brown et al., 2009), as well as molecular changes in spinal glial cells (Chen et al., 2020). Such changes in the spinal cells would, in turn, influence the myelin sheaths of local muscle cells that are traced to the spinal cord, midbrain, and hypothalamus/pituitary axis (Ezzo & Streitberger, 2006.). One study of Emotional Freedom Techniques (EFT) of veterans found epigenetic changes in genes related to inflammation and immunity (Church et al., 2018).

EFT makes reference to the meridian system of acupoints, articulated by TCM. In contrast, AIT references the chakra system. The seven primary chakras are located within the nervous system, in both the brain and the spine (Malimas et al., 2023). They are connected with a complex series of pathways that move energy throughout the body, called *nadis,* which means "little rivers." The three main nadis located on the centerline of the body are correlated to the central nervous system of the spinal cord and the autonomic nervous systems (sympathetic and parasympathetic; Agrawal et al., 2021).

Chakras are traditionally conceptualized as discs of energy that move (spin) to support the flow of energy within the individual. Nadis are pathways within the chakra system that guide the energetic information from chakras throughout the body. Historically, there has been concern about differentiating between the meridians of TCM and chakras; however, modern researchers are beginning to correlate meridians with the nadis of the chakra system (Niharika et al., 2013). This integration may suggest the movement toward a more cohesive model between these two systems (Jun et al., 2020).

The chakra system was introduced in India from tantric yoga traditions (Feuerstein, 2001). It was used as a guide for practitioners to attain higher states of consciousness and health (Motoyama, 2003). Then in 1879, Helena Blavatsky of the Theosophical Society introduced chakras to Western thought. The chakra system has continued to influence thought through the human potential movement, through the work of Ram Dass and Abraham Maslow in the 1960s and 1970s (Leland, 2017). The early 20th-century Western hypothesis that the chakras are associated with specific mood states and developmental tasks originated with psychiatrist Carl Jung (1996). His work was simplified as a map for psychological healing and personal development later in the century (Judith, 2004).

Further research established that chakras could be delineated and perhaps correlated to human anatomy and physiology, which provided a foundation for biofield-based therapies (Gerber, 2000). Motoyama (1981) documented that chakras emit photoelectric and high-frequency oscillations when activated. Likewise, Hunt and colleagues (1977) documented distinct chakric frequency bands between 100 Hz and 1 KHz.

The 21st-century hypothesis suggests that chakras are central to human health and well-being. It further suggests that the chakras are accessible to human awareness. Ultimately, Moga (2022) concluded that there is enough evidence regarding chakras to warrant further study, rather than dismissing the idea.

Studies by Rokade (2017) and Sweta et al. (2018) correlated the heart and root chakras to major neurological plexuses, supporting the hypothesis of neuroanatomical impact. Rowold and Hewson (2020) confirmed Hunt's (1977) frequency bands and found two more for a total of 10. Jalil et al. (2015) found that each chakra radiates a unique band of frequencies from 29 MHz to 86 MHz, with the highest frequencies found at the third eye and crown chakras.

While originally housed in spiritual practices, chakras also provide an interoceptive map to the central nervous system (Loizzo, 2016). They do not require accommodation in traditional biophysics (Kafatos et al., 2015; Srinivasan, 2010).

While the research of chakra systems falls short of that related to meridians, the emerging data have identified further interventions and mechanisms of change in several areas: physiology (Rokade, 2017; Sweta et al., 2018), neuroscience (Phillips et al., 2020), microbiology (Movaffaghi & Mohammad, 2009), neurobiology (Maxwell, 2009), obstetrics and gynecology (Huang, 2020), embryogenesis (Balkrishna et al., 2018) and human and artificial consciousness (Chaturvedi, 2019; Cooper et al., 2020).

Memory Reconsolidation

Psychotherapist Bruce Ecker (2012, 2015) introduced a biologically based discussion of how negative emotions attached to a traumatic memory become stored in the brain, as applied to psychotherapeutic intervention. He elucidated a sequence of psychotherapeutic events by which the intensity of that emotion could be substantially reduced or extinguished.

The sequential requirements include: first, bringing into awareness the memory trace connected to the negative emotion; second, changing the physiological state such that the new positive emotional state (parasympathetic) is no longer compatible with the original negative emotional state (sympathetic) while the aspects of the memory trace remain in awareness; and third, allowing the memory to return to long-term memory storage while maintaining its new association with the positive emotion.

This general sequence of events in the therapeutic process provides a neurobiological account for what can at times be a dramatic change in emotional tone achieved in therapy, such as in EMDR, as well as in certain forms of hypnosis, classical behaviorism as applied, and Energy Psychology. This is a general mechanism not specific to a particular psychotherapeutic technique.

Functional MRI scans have demonstrated a unique role of dual attentional awareness and/or bifocal processing in successfully processing and extinguishing negative emotions associated with traumatic memory (Wittfoth et al., 2020). The physical sensation of tapping in EFT, combined with the memory trace, is thought to create a dual level of attention that aids in the processing of phobic stimuli. Bifocal processing in AIT would involve the physical sensation of hand placement at various points of the body, while focusing on the memory or trauma.

Parts Integration

AIT theorizes that a person is composed of three structural parts: the conscious self, the body, and the ego, which governs the former two parts. In addition, there is the unconscious self, and beneath that, the client's Center, which is their own deepest, wisest Self. Clinicians utilize AIT to support the client in connecting to their own Center (Clinton, 2010). "The ego is connected to the Center by a bridge through which questions, prayer, information, experience, inspiration, wisdom, guidance, emotion, creativity, and much more, can be communicated. This connection is called the Ego-Center Bridge" (Clinton, 2010, p. 63).

AIT also includes references to "aligning the client's being for transformation." This is based on the therapeutic assumption that traumatized persons do not achieve lasting relief from their trauma symptoms because there are "unconscious" parts that prevent release of stored trauma (Clinton, 2010).

In the early phase of treatment, AIT practitioners identify and extinguish clients' core beliefs that may block the progress of therapy. This initial phase is referred to as the Alliance, or the Agreement, and it is designed to bring conscious and unconscious perspectives into alignment in support of growth and change (Clinton, 2010).

Through the client befriending and integrating these "parts," the client is able to live more fully in the present. The Internal Family Systems Theory articulates that different parts of the person can split off as a result of the need to cope with circumstances of early life. These parts, labeled as protector parts, function as the building blocks to healing in the present day (Anderson et al., 2017). By finding relief and peace from the negative thoughts, feelings, sensations, and memories from early periods of life, AIT allows clients to integrate all their parts to live as a whole version of themselves in their present-day lives.

Information Reprocessing

Eye Movement Desensitization and Reprocessing (EMDR) has demonstrated effects beyond that of medication in the treatment of PTSD (van der Kolk et al., 2007). EMDR posits that traumatic events become "stuck" in the brain and body as memories, sensations, emotions, and cognitions. Utilizing bilateral stimulation allows the client to desensitize and reprocess these traumatic events so that one may remember the experience with a more tolerable and neutral state of mind, without the distressful emotions and sensations attached to the original memory (Shapiro, 2001).

Bilateral stimulation can be visual, tactile, or auditory. The specific mechanism of action underlying the dual attention stimuli/alternating bilateral stimulation (DAS/ABS) element of EMDR therapy is highly debated. Psychiatrist Paul Miller in the *Journal of Medical Hypotheses* opines that DAS/ABS allows for a "stochastic resonance" or "white noise" effect that can allow stored traumas to enter conscious awareness and then be desensitized, reprocessed, and released (Miller et al., 2018).

AIT also utilizes DAS in that it incorporates tactile stimulation of different parts of the body while verbally repeating the treatment phrase out loud. While EMDR utilizes side-to-side bilateral stimulation (BLS), AIT utilizes top-to-bottom tactile stimulation, starting at the crown of the head and ending at the base of the tailbone, also known as the "root" energy center. AIT's hand movement gives the client the cue on where to put the focus on their body and to bring their attention to emotions or sensations that arise when they repeat the treatment statement at each energy center (Clinton, 2010). The basic protocols of both AIT and EMDR combine a form of treatment phrase with the DAS/ABS.

Embodiment and Dissociation Treatment

"Traumatic symptoms are not caused by the 'triggering' event itself. They stem from the frozen residue of energy that had not been resolved or discharged; this residue remains trapped in the nervous system where it can wreak havoc on our bodies and spirits."
—Peter Levine (1997, p. 3)

One of the most promising aspects of somatic therapies such as AIT is its capacity to treat dissociative disorders. Dissociation is a common symptom in patients with trauma, especially attachment traumas of neglect or abuse (van der Kolk, 2015).

In *The Body Keeps the Score*, van der Kolk (2015) states that some of the most difficult clients to treat are those that numbed into hypo-arousal, commonly referred to as the "freeze response." These clients may be difficult to recognize as dissociated, especially if dissociation is adaptive in their present-day lives.

Common clinical presentations include: operating on "autopilot," not feeling present in daily life, shutting down in the face of conflict, difficulty with identifying emotions, flat affect, memory loss, emotions of sadness and despair, physical symptoms of exhaustion and burnout, and social withdrawal. Psychologist Sandra Paulsen describes these clients as presenting in therapy with the "front porch" of the self. These clients appear to be able to engage in traditional talk therapy but do not receive lasting benefits because they are only performing the actions they believe to be required of them. This is a recreation of patterns that created safety for them in childhood.

Clients who experience traumatic dissociation can attend "talk" psychotherapy for years without experiencing relief from their dissociative symptoms and their deepest traumas (Paulsen & O'Shea, 2017). In our experience, a gentle somatic therapy such as AIT may provide an effective means of treating trauma-related dissociation.

Gently returning the client's focus to the body provides the controlled desensitization to the threat response evoked by traumatic memories. The function of this embodiment is to show, not tell, the client that while their nervous system experiences emotional discomfort, there is no actual danger in the present. This can be done before treating traumatic memories as a way to build distress tolerance in AIT.

Historical Elements

Psychiatrist Carl Jung devoted his career to the development of a depth psychology, which he entitled "analytic psychology" to differentiate it from Freud's psychoanalysis. Jung referenced a larger sense of wholeness internalized within each individual. He described this inner awareness to be the experience of the divine image, which he referred to as the Self.

This definition of the term "Self" is substantially different from that associated with self-psychology or object relations theory. This internal awareness of the complete wholeness of a person as a reflection of the introjected sense of the divine was the completion of what Jung called the "individuation process," which was the goal of therapy.

The process required a series of steps that involved integration of what is perceived to be another "part" of consciousness, separate from the ego. Examples include integration of the shadow into the ego, and later the integration of the contrasexual element of the psyche known as the *anima* or *animus*. The latter integration opens the ego-Self axis and thus appreciation of this larger sense of being.

Much of this language is preserved in AIT, although the term Self is replaced with the term Center. AIT also references internal archetypes including the shadow, anima, and animus in various protocols available. Asha Clinton specifically references Jung and his work as helping inform some of the concepts of AIT (Edinger, 1992; Jung, 1969; Wilmer, 2018.).

The philosophy of AIT assumes that archetypes are universal and part of the collective unconscious, such that each person is born with the full panoply of archetypes (Clinton, 2020). Through life experiences, the qualities of archetypes and their opposites are activated and/or introjected and shape personality and meaning-making.

A Jungian practice used by AIT that impacts client experience and autonomy is the use of active imagination both within and outside of the session. Active imagination (AI) is used by the client within session to identify cognitive and somatic structures that are attached to traumatic experiences. Outside of sessions, the client uses AI for additional self-exploration.

AIT additionally provides a set of meditations for home practice to install positive patterning for use in meditation or the de-escalation of triggered experiencing and activation (Clinton et al., 2014).

Energy Psychology

AIT credits Thought Field Therapy, created by Roger Callahan (1985), for the innovative applications of kinesiology and for the recognition and extinguishing of "psychological reversals" prior to treatment of trauma. Emotional Freedom Techniques, developed from TFT by Gary Craig (Craig & Fowlie, 1985), is credited for the format of the Quick AIT Protocol, as well as the integration of elements of exposure therapy with memory, emotion, and bodily sensation.

AIT's Areas of Focus

AIT has multiple applications that allow for the processing of either single events or more sophisticated patterns of events. When working with patterns, many individual events may be efficiently extinguished at the same time.

The first and most straightforward use of AIT would be to extinguish the negative emotions related to single events. The general sequence described in the basic manual (Clinton, 2010) is termed a "three step" and involves performing the AIT sequence on the first historical event with a similar emotional tone (Originating Trauma), followed by the current event (Initiating Trauma), and then their connection (Connecting Trauma).

Traumatic events can lead a person to develop a negative belief about themselves or the world as a compensatory response. AIT provides a protocol to eliminate negative underlying beliefs followed by a strengthening of a positive belief. This process is identified in the Core Belief Matrices (Clinton, 2018). This process is not entirely dissimilar from the EMDR process of identifying a negative core belief and replacing it with a positive one.

The specific verbiage used in AIT therapy may account for its ability to extinguish patterns of events that occurred over the course of a lifetime. The language phrase for this is "all the times and all the ways I felt X when Y happened to me, up until now." This phrasing is unique with AIT and allows for the conscious mind to enlist the subconscious and unconscious mind to filter entire sequences of events of this pattern, thereby providing a substantial symptom relief (Clinton, 2010). It also provides efficiency in real time.

AIT offers the capacity for the individual to install positive belief structures. Clients are encouraged to practice it daily at home between sessions once a positive belief is identified (Clinton, 2010).

The Quick AIT Protocol is a rapid extinguishing mechanism clients can use on their own between sessions to reduce negative emotions that arise. The Quick AIT format is discussed in the following section and is similar in format to EFT (Clinton, 2010).

The Basic Process of Quick AIT

Either while in session or independently, Quick AIT is a simple process that can be easily learned and used. Each energy center is related to a chakra and has a specific hand placement, as illustrated in Figure 1.

The Quick AIT Protocol

1. The client chooses a memory, aspect, emotion, somatic experience, etc. (now called issue) they would like to treat. The client is instructed to focus on the chosen issue and to remember relevant details, including any emotions and sensations. They are encouraged to allow the emotion or sensory experience to arise to awareness.
2. The client uses a SUD scale of 0 to 10 to describe their current level of distress and the client's answer is always accepted.
3. The client is instructed to treat any reversals they intuit or expect by massaging their "sore points" located on the chest wall beneath the hollow of the throat and 3 inches on each side of the sternum centerline. Basics text: first find the little indentation at the base of the throat. From that point, bring your fingers out about 3 inches to each side.
4. The client states a short phrase that summarizes the facts of the current issue. This phrase will be repeated internally or spoken at each energy center listed in this process.
5. The client identifies the location to which they will hold a hand throughout the protocol. This is called the stationary hand; the client may switch hands if they choose to do so. The ideal energy center to hold is frequently the one closest to the epicenter of somatic disruption or discomfort.
6. The client will guide the non-stationary hand through each of the energy centers from the crown of the head to the base

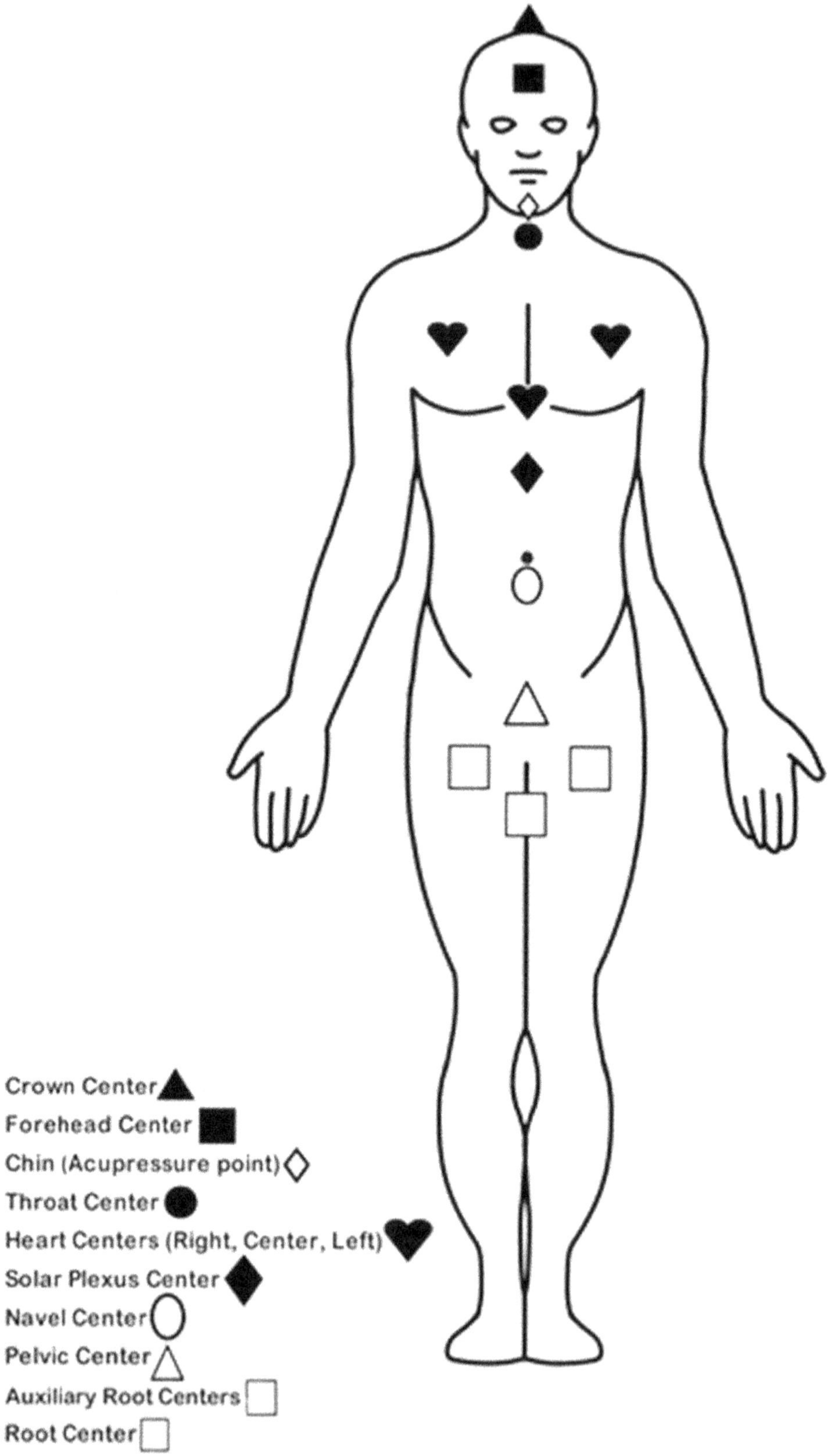

Figure 1. Energy centers used in AIT (illustration by Paul Weaver, 2021).

of the spine while repeating the chosen phrase at each center.

7. To guide and mirror the client, the clinician (when in session) will also hold the energy centers on the clinician's body as the client holds theirs, beginning with the crown energy center. Each energy center is held for the length of at least one breath.
8. After one round (the previous sequence) is completed, the client will take a grounding or extinguishing breath, then return their focus to the chosen issue and to their current emotional and sensory experience. They will then use the SUD scale to score their current distress level. Further intervention is based on their SUD assessment as follows:
   a. If there is a reduction of 2 points or more but has not yet gone down to 0, do another round.
   b. If there is a reduction of 1 point or less, or if the SUD has gone up, rub the sore spots for about 2 minutes to correct any potential lingering psychological reversals.
   c. If treatment for reversals does not improve the SUD score sufficiently, the client should investigate whether another aspect of the issue has come up.
      i. If another aspect has emerged and the SUD rating of the original memory is now 2 or less, it is appropriate to redirect focus to the new aspect and begin another round of treatment.
      ii. If the SUD level of the original memory is above 2, it is best for the client to complete further treatment rounds on the original memory until the SUD is 2 or less, and then switch to the new aspect.
   d. If the client reports a lingering SUD level of 1, repeat the phrase a few times with one hand on the stationary energy center and the other on another energy center as identified by the client as a secondary point or per clinical judgment. A full round is not necessary if the SUD level reaches 0.
   e. The client completes the number of rounds necessary for the issue and its aspects to reach a SUD level of 0.
9. When the client's SUD level has reached 0, offer gratitude for the change by saying "Hallelujah!" or an equivalent.

The Larger Vision of the Complete AIT Process

Gaining Alliance

The Alliance/Agreement: One of the basic protocols that AIT clinicians receive in their training and are encouraged to utilize with clients early in treatment is the "Agreement Protocol." It is a list of 24 core beliefs, which could be described as "blocking beliefs." These beliefs such as, "It's impossible to be healed" or "It's not safe to be healed," are described by Clinton (2010) as needing to be "used at the beginning of treatment to ensure that the client's underlying unconscious beliefs about healing and transformation are positive before treatment is begun."

Any therapist who works with trauma and dissociation knows that there are clients who are afraid, and sometimes even certain, that treatment will not work. Many clients are anxious that trauma treatment will make them feel worse than they do already. Extinguishing blocking beliefs, such as "I'll be deprived if I'm healed," allow the client and therapist to clear the way for a conscious, unconscious, and embodied agreement that healing and transformation are possible, desirable, and deserved (Clinton, 2010).

Aligning Being for Transformation

After treating, or extinguishing, these blocking beliefs and working to strengthen their healthy opposites (e.g., from "I must be perfect" to an adaptive belief "It's plenty good enough to be human"), the client is ready to align all systems in their body for transformation. This includes making the agreement that their unconscious self is willing to allow them to use AIT to heal all the wounds they choose to heal in different systems in their body, for example, the musculoskeletal system or the nervous system. The language is about agreement and consent, making note that the client is allowing for AIT to heal all the wounds they choose to heal. For those clients that have struggled with dissociation, trauma splitting, or having maladaptive coping strategies or "protector parts," letting the client discern what they are ready to release and what they do not choose to change may be quite empowering.

Protocols: Mastering AIT Practice

An addition to Basic AIT, there is a manualized set of treatment approaches for complex issues. The use of protocols and matrices allows

AIT practitioners to access a skill set for treating early attachment rupture and other traumas from early life prior to the development of clear language capacity. Other protocols allow for the treatment of ancestral or intergenerational trauma, which may not be linked to explicit personal memories, but instead may be linked to somatic consequences in the body.

Case Example

A client presented to the clinician (author E.P.) after his previous therapist retired. He requested therapy related to grief issues surrounding his father's death from amyotrophic lateral sclerosis when the client was 12 years old. After 10 sessions of talk therapy, including history taking and five sessions of AIT in a period of three months, the client's Dissociative Experiences Scale (DES-II) score was reduced by 53.6% from 43.93 to 20.36. At six-month follow-up after 14 sessions of AIT, the client's DES-II score reduced by 61%, from 20.36 to 7.86, which is essentially a normal score found in the general population (Carlson & Putnam, 1993). At nine-month follow-up, the client's DES II scores rose to 11.07. The total change in his DES-II scores over nine months of AIT was 32.86 points, a 74.8% decrease in symptom severity.

The client reported that he had been in talk therapy for years but had been unable to find adequate relief from his trauma because he was unaware he was dissociating. The patient also shared his perspective on AIT and how it differs from traditional talk therapy. He was previously in talk therapy for five years.

> It [AIT] has this somatic component, moving through the stations on the body, that has a very real effect of pulling me out of the fear rising from my thoughts, feelings and emotions. It feels like direct access to my feelings. Sometimes in talk therapy it felt like I was talking in loops. The structure of AIT also pulls me out of that rumination cycle that I would get into in talk therapy. In AIT, it always feels like we're moving through things, which is satisfying to me. In my talk therapy, there was a focus on what I thought about things. And in AIT, there's a focus on how I feel. This is a paradigm shift for me in my life and experience. (Transcript of Session #72)

Learning More

As there are substantially fewer AIT practitioners than other modes of Energy Psychology, those interested may consult the Advanced Integrative Therapy Institute (AITI) website, where a full series of basic and advanced course material is on the calendar. Hands-on experience with at least a basic level of training in AIT is the most effective way to learn the technique. In addition, the website for the Association for Comprehensive Energy Psychology (ACEP) has a complete list of all the research conducted in Energy Psychology from the 1990s to the present. This includes article citations related to AIT. To find a practitioner of AIT, there is a partial list at the AITI website. Additionally, many practitioners will list this modality in their listing site at the ACEP website.

Discussion

This article attempts to describe the history, foundation, and scope of practice of AIT, from the theoretical to the practical. AIT has evolved from a variety of philosophies and treatment models ranging from Jung's analytical psychology to EFT to elements of somatic therapy and kinesiology. As there is currently a shortage of peer-reviewed research conducted on AIT, the general purpose of this article was to define and thereby introduce AIT to fellow researchers, clinical mental health professionals, and laypersons.

Salient information that emerged from the present review includes: (a) what AIT is, including one treatment protocol; (b) a review of the small body of peer-reviewed literature and studies that are currently published about AIT; (c) proposed mechanisms for action of the body-based/energy component; and (d) the obvious need for more research studies to be conducted on the efficacy of AIT as an effective trauma treatment.

The current working hypothesis for AIT's mechanism of action may be subject to change as more research is conducted into this therapeutic intervention. It is certainly beyond the scope of this article to defend scientifically the existence of chakras, and the authors acknowledge that more data exist related to meridian systems in the literature. The possible correlations between the nadis as energy channels connecting chakras to the body and the meridian-based TCM system is an intriguing possibility for potential integration of models, at least in theory.

Although AIT uses the language of chakras to facilitate the therapeutic process, it may be found that its effectiveness is in part due to split awareness, memory reconsolidation, somatic processing, bilateral stimulation, or any number of potential considerations. The question of the cause of effect deserves considerable attention and future research. Before Alexander Fleming knew how penicillin worked, he was aware it was effective in curbing the growth of bacteria (Tan & Tatsumura, 2015). How AIT works will continue to become clearer as thorough research that includes biometric measures is conducted into this treatment method.

EFT, which is an evidence-based Energy Psychology treatment method, emerged into the public consciousness as a result of extensive peer-reviewed studies and an ever-growing body of research with over 100 studies demonstrating its efficacy (Bach et al., 2019). Research into the effectiveness of AIT is in its nascence, but thanks to past and ongoing research conducted in other Energy Psychology methods there is a research "roadmap" on how to proceed. The potential for future research into AIT appears promising.

The richness of the model and the preliminary results of the few case studies and a survey of therapists (Brown et al., 2022) suggest that this modality deserves substantial additional study. Coauthor G.B. is currently conducting a randomized clinical trial (RCT) comparing EFT and the Quick AIT Protocol to further develop data. This trial also includes the biometric measure of heart rate variability.

Additional case studies and RCTs comparing AIT with trauma-focused cognitive behavioral therapy or EMDR could further assess the effectiveness of this relatively novel Energy Psychology method.

Conclusion

Dr. Asha Clinton is quoted as saying, "Trauma is anything that fractures human wholeness." As clinicians, the authors of this article recognize that the need for gentle, effective, and evidence-based trauma treatment methods has never been more urgent. Although AIT is in its infancy and much more clinical experience and research are required, the initial data provide some optimism. The most obvious limitation of this review is the meager amount of research data currently available regarding AIT. The function of this paper is to garner interest into AIT, as well as to open up avenues for further research.

References

Agrawal, G. A., Upadhyay, S., & Sakshi. (2021). Study of Trividha Nadis; Ida, Pingala and Sushumna Nadi: A Review Article. *World Journal of Pharmaceutical and Medical Research, 7*(2), 555694.

Anderson, F., Sweezy, M., & Schwartz, R. (2017). *Internal family systems skills training manual trauma-informed treatment for anxiety, depression, PTSD and substance abuse.* PESI Publishing & Media.

Bach, D., Groesbeck, G., Stapleton, P., Banton, S., Blickheuser, K., & Church, D. (2019). Clinical EFT (Emotional Freedom Techniques) improves multiple physiological markers of health. *Journal of Evidence-Based Integrative Medicine, 24.* doi:10.1177/2515690X18823691

Balkrishna, A., Sharma, V. K., & Sharma, N. (2018). Chakra genesis, a correlation between evolution of chakras and embryogenesis. *Journal of Yoga and Physiotherapy ISSN,* 2476–1303. doi:10.19080/JYP.2018.06.555694

Bird Weaver, T. (2021). The use of Advanced Integrative Therapy with C-PTSD and intergenerational trauma transmission: A case study. *Energy Psychology: Theory, Research, and Treatment, 13*(2), 23–38. doi:10.9769/EPJ.2021.13.2.TBW

Brown, C. A., & Jones, A. K. (2009). Physiological mechanisms of acupuncture: Beyond placebo? *Pain, 147*(1), 11–12. doi:10.1016/j.pain.2009.09.014

Brown, G. P., Batra, K., Hong, S. S., Sottile, R., Bakhru, R., & Dorin, E. (2022). Therapists' observations in reduction of unpleasant emotions following Advanced Integrative Therapy interventions. *Energy Psychology: Theory, Research, and Treatment, 14*(1), 12–21. doi:10.9769/EPJ.2022.14.1.GB

Callahan, R. (1985). *Five minute phobia cure: Dr. Callahan's treatment for fears, phobias, and self-sabotage.* Enterprise.

Carlson, E. B., & Putnam, F. W. (1993). An update on the dissociative experiences scale. *Dissociation: Progress in the Dissociative Disorders, 6*(1), 16–27.

Chaturvedi, D. K. (2019). Relationship between chakra energy and consciousness. *Biomedical Journal of Science and Technical Research, 15*(3), 1–3.

Chen, T., Zhang, W. W., Chu, Y. X., & Wang, Y. Q. (2020). Acupuncture for pain management: Molecular mechanisms of action. *American Journal of Chinese Medicine, 48*(4), 793–811. doi:10.1142/S0192415X20500408

Church, D., Yount, G., & Brooks, A. J. (2012). The effect of Emotional Freedom Techniques on stress biochemistry: A randomized controlled trial. *Journal of Nervous and Mental Disease, 200*(10), 891–896. doi:10.1097/NMD.0b013e31826b9fc1

Church, D., Yount, G., Rachlin, K., Fox, L., & Nelms, J. (2018). Epigenetic effects of PTSD remediation in veterans using clinical Emotional Freedom Techniques: A randomized controlled pilot study. *American Journal of Health Promotion, 32*(1), 112–122. doi:10.1177/0890117116661154

Clinton, A. (2010). *Advanced Integrative Therapy: The basics.* Advanced Integrative Therapy Institute.

Clinton, A. (2018). *The AIT core belief book: All the cognitions you'll ever need to promote transformation and healing.* Advanced Integrative Therapy Institute.

Clinton, A. (2020). *Depth treatment* (5th ed.). Advanced Integrative Therapy Institute.

Clinton, A., Folkers, C., & Soberman, G. (2014). *Mastering AIT practice* (5th ed.). Advanced Integrative Therapy Institute.

Cloitre, M., Shevlin, M., Brewin, C., Bisson, J., Roberts, N., Maercker, A., Karatzias, T., & Hyland, P. (2018). The International Trauma Questionnaire: Development of a self-report measure of ICD-11 PTSD and Complex PTSD. *Acta Psychiatrica Scandinavica, 138*(6), 536–546. doi:10.1111/acps.12956

Cooper, N., Clarkson, J., Phillips, K. T., & Hall, C. J. (2020). Consciousness and the Amit Ray's quantum attention function of the brain. *Brain, 6,* 14. doi:10.13140/RG.2.2.24159.48805

Craig, G., & Fowlie, A. (1995). *Emotional Freedom Techniques: The manual.* Gary Craig.

Ecker, B. (2012). *Unlocking the emotional brain: Eliminating symptoms at their roots using memory reconsolidation.* Routledge.

Ecker, B. (2015). *Memory reconsolidation in psychotherapy: The neuropsychotherapist special issue.* CreateSpace.

Edinger, E. (1992). *Ego and archetype.* Shambhala.

Elliott, R. (2014). Hermeneutic single-case efficacy design. In K. Schneider, J. Pierson, & J. Bugental (Eds.), *The handbook of humanistic psychology: Theory, research, and practice* (2nd ed., pp. 351–360). Sage.

Elliott, R., Slatick, E., & Urman, M. (2001). Qualitative change process research on psychotherapy: Alternative strategies. In J. Frömmer and D. L. Rennie (Eds.), *Qualitative psychotherapy research: Methods and methodology* (pp. 69–111). Pabst Science.

Ezzo, J., Streitberger, K., & Schneider, A. (2006). Cochrane systematic reviews examine P6 acupuncture-point stimulation for nausea and vomiting. *Journal of Alternative and Complementary Medicine, 12*(5), 489–495.

Feuerstein, G. (2001). *The yoga tradition: Its history, literature, philosophy and practice.* Hohm.

Folkers, C. (Ed.). (2022). *Treating trauma with energy psychology.* Outskirts.

Gerber, R. (2000). *Vibrational medicine for the 21st century: A complete guide to energy healing and spiritual transformation.* William Morrow.

Huang, W. L. (2020). Chakra's energy deficiency as the main cause of infertility in women. *Obstetrics and Gynecology International Journal, 11*(2), 83–91. doi:10.15406/ogij.2020.11.00493

Hunt, V., Massey, W., Weinberg, R., & Hahn, P. (1977). A study of structural integration from neuromuscular, energy field, and emotional approaches. *Bulletin of Structural Integration, 5,* 19–37.

Irgens, A. C., Hoffart, A., Nysæter, T., Haaland, V. Ø., Borge, F., Pripp, A. H., Martinsen, E. W., & Dammen, T. (2017). Thought field therapy compared to cognitive behavioral therapy and wait-list for agoraphobia: A randomized, controlled study with a 12-month follow-up. *Frontiers in Psychology, 8,* 1027. doi:10.3389/fpsyg.2017.01027

Jalil, S. Z. A., Abdullah, H., & Taib, M. N. (2015). Detection of endogenous electromagnetic field of the human body. *ARPN Journal of Engineering Applied Sciences, 10*(20), 9650–9658.

Judith A. (2004). *Eastern body, western mind: Psychology and the chakra system as a path to the self.* Celestial Arts.

Jun, F., Bok, B. H., & Lin, Z. (2020). Study on the correlations between chakra system and ayurvedic medicine. *International Journal of Ayurveda and Pharma Research, 8*(4), 73–76.

Jung, C. G. (1969). *Man and his symbols.* Doubleday.

Jung, C. G. (1996). *The psychology of kundalini yoga: Notes of a seminar by C. G. Jung, with S. Shamdasani.* Princeton University Press.

Kafatos, M. C., Chevalier, G., Chopra, D., Hubacher, J., Kak, S., & Theise, N. D. (2015). Biofield science: Current physics perspectives. *Global Advances in Health and Medicine,* 4(1_suppl), 25–34. doi:10.7453/gahmj.2015.011.suppl

Kuhfuß, M., Maldei, T., Hetmanek, A., & Baumann, N. (2021). Somatic experiencing—effectiveness and key factors of a body-oriented trauma therapy: A scoping literature review. *European Journal of Psychotraumatology, 12*(1), 1–17. doi:10.1080/20008198.2021.1929023

Leland, K. (2017). The rainbow body: How the western chakra system came to be. *Quest, 105.2,* 25–29.

Levine, P. A. (1997). *Waking the tiger: Healing trauma—the innate capacity to transform overwhelming experiences.* North Atlantic Books.

Llewelyn, S. P., Elliott, R., Shapiro, D. A., Hardy, G., & Firth-Cozens, J. (1988). Client perceptions of significant events in prescriptive and exploratory periods of individual therapy. *British Journal of Clinical Psychology, 27*(2), 105–114. doi:10.1111/j.2044-8260.1988.tb00758.x

Loizzo, J. (2016). The subtle body: An interoceptive map of central nervous system function and meditative mind-brain-body integration. *Annals of the New York Academy of Sciences, 1373*(1), 78–95. doi:10.1111/nyas.13065

Malimas, S., Yosravikul, K., Jiarawattananon, M., & Makmoon, T., Khiwwichai, R., Raksakorn, I., … Saokarn, A. (2023). Exploring the interconnection between chakras and the nervous system through the Buddhist meditation approach and a revised understanding of the chakras system. *International Journal of Novel Research in Healthcare and Nursing, 10*(1), 140–145. doi:10.5281/zenodo.7821110

Maxwell, R. W. (2009). Neurobiology of chakras and prayer. *Zygon, 44*(4).

Miller, P. W., McGowan, I. W., Bergmann, U., Farrell, D., & McLaughlin, D. F. (2018). Stochastic resonance as a proposed neurobiological model for Eye Movement Desensitization and Reprocessing (EMDR) therapy. *Medical Hypotheses, 121,* 106–111. doi:10.1016/j.mehy.2018.09.010

Moga, Margaret. (2022). Is there scientific evidence for chakras? *International Journal of Healing and Caring, 22*(2), 39–45.

Motoyama, H. (1981). *Theories of the chakras: Bridge to higher consciousness.* Theosophical Publishing House.

Motoyama, H. (2003). *Theories of the chakras: Bridge to higher consciousness.* New Age Books.

Movaffaghi, Z., & Mohammad, F. (2009). Biofield therapies: Biophysical basis and biological regulation? *Complementary Therapies in Clinical Practice, 15*(1), 35–37.

Nelms, J., & Castel, D. (2016). A systematic review and meta-analysis of randomized and non-randomized trials of Emotional Freedom Techniques (EFT) for the treatment of depression. *Explore: The Journal of Science and Healing, 12*(6), 416–426. doi:10.1016/j.explore.2016.08.001

Niharika, N., Hankey, A., & Nagendra, H. R. (2013). Effects of yoga practice on acumeridian energies: Variance reduction implies benefits for regulation. *International Journal of Yoga, 6*(1), 61–65.

Pace, E. (2021). Efficacy of Advanced Integrative Therapy in treating complex post traumatic stress disorder: A preliminary case report. *International Journal of Healing and Caring, 21*(2), 35–53.

Paulsen, S., & O'Shea, K. (2017). *When there are no words: Repairing early trauma and neglect from the attachment period with EMDR Therapy.* CreateSpace.

Phillips, K., & Cooper, N. J., Hall, C., & Clarkson, J. (2020). Neuroscience and neuropsychology models of brain based on Saint Amit Ray's 114-chakra system. *Neuropsychology Review Journal, 9*(27), 1–10. doi:10.13140/RG.2.2.26134.57927

Pianta, R. (1992). *Child-Parent Relationship Scale (CPRS).* Retrieved from https://education.virginia.edu/faculty-research/centers-labs-projects/castl/measures-developed-robert-c-pianta-phd

Rankin, L. (2022). *Sacred medicine: A doctor's quest to unravel the mysteries of healing.* Sounds True.

Rokade, S. D. (2017). Role of anahata chakra and cardiac plexus in cardiac activity. *Indian Journal of Medical Research Pharmaceutical Sciences, 4*(1), 23–26.

Rowold, J., & Hewson, P. D. (2020). Biofield frequency bands—Definitions and group differences. *Global Advances Health Medicine, 9,* 1–10.

Shapiro, F. (2001). *Eye Movement Desensitization and Reprocessing (EMDR): Basic principles, protocols, and procedures.* Guilford.

Srinivasan, T. M. (2010). Energy medicine [editorial]. *International Journal of Yoga, 3,* 1.

Sweta, K. M., Awasthi, H. H., Godbole, A., & Prajapati, S. (2018). Physio-anatomical resemblance of inferior hypogastric plexus with muladhara chakra: A cadaveric study. *AYU International Quarterly Journal of Research in Ayurveda, 38*(1–2), 7–9.

Tan, S. Y., & Tatsumura, Y. (2015). Alexander Fleming (1881–1955): Discoverer of penicillin. *Singapore Medical Journal, 56*(7), 366–367. doi:10.11622/smedj.2015105

van der Kolk, B. (2015). *The body keeps the score: Brain, mind, and body in the healing of trauma.* Penguin.

van der Kolk, B. A., Spinazzola, J., Blaustein, M. E., Hopper, J. W., Hopper, E. K., Korn, D. L., & Simpson, W. B. (2007). A randomized clinical trial of eye movement desensitization, fluoxetine, and pill placebo in the treatment of posttraumatic stress disorder: Treatment effects and long-term maintenance. *Journal of Clinical Psychiatry, 68*(1), 37.

Weathers, F., Litz, B., Keane, T., Palmieri, P., Marx, B., & Schnurr, P. P. (2013). *The PTSD Checklist for DSM-5 (PCL-5).* Retrieved from https://www.ptsd.va.gov/professional/assessment/documents/PCL5_Standard_form

Wilmer, H. (2018). *Practical Jung: Nuts and bolts of Jungian psychotherapy.* Chiron.

Wittfoth, D., Pfeiffer, A., Bohne, M., Lanfermann, H., & Wittfoth, M. (2020). Emotion regulation through bifocal processing of fear inducing and disgust inducing stimuli. *BMC Neuroscience, 21*(1), 1–13. doi:10.1186/s12868-020-00597-x

Wolpe, J. (1969). *The practice of behavior therapy.* Pergamon Press.

World Health Organization (WHO). (2021). 6B41 Complex post traumatic stress disorder. *International classification of diseases 11th revision.* Retrieved from https://icd.who.int

If you would like to write book reviews for Energy Psychology *journal, we'd love to hear from you. Get inspiring books for free! Contact Stephanie Marohn at angel@stephaniemarohn.com*

IntraConnected: MWe (Me + We) as the Integration of Self, Identity, and Belonging

Daniel J. Siegel, MD

W. W. Norton, 2022
Softcover, 336 Pages
$29.99
ISBN: 978-0393711691

Reviewed by Carol A. Atkinson

In today's global wave of me against the other, Daniel Seigel's book *IntraConnected* uses the neurobiology of human maturation, Indigenous perspectives, and contemplative teachings as a way to call Earth's citizens to a greater connectedness and union.

Seigel admits to a life of privilege—white, male, from a well-educated family of means. Without one defining moment in his teens, he may not have been open to understanding humans' connectedness. He wrote of a time in his teens when he went on a mission trip to Mexico. He was riding a horse when the saddle loosened and his body and the saddle went under the horse's belly. His feet were caught in the stirrups and the horse ran even faster with its unbalanced load. The boy's head and back bounced against the stone-strewn path, his body pummeled by the frightened horse. Seigel said that, as he came into consciousness afterward, he had no idea who he was and everything seemed to be a seamless whole, dazzlingly beautiful, and shimmering with light. It was only after he began to recover and remembered his name and who he was that he realized he had experienced something beyond his self. As he matured into his medical professional, mostly linear life, he began to learn how that teenage neurobiological event had occurred (allowing his brain to function in wholeness rather than separation) and to understand the wholeness within quantum physics and the meaning of complex systems theory.

Quantum physics taught him of a world of "verb-like" happenings among the quanta (small units of energy) that were deeply connected (p. 32). Here were only emerging events where time and space did not exist to create a sense of separation (p. 32). Systems theory also revealed a way to understand connections and patterns in how the individual parts actually are related—"it's about relationality, not individuality alone" (p. 32). Those defining concepts, coupled with his study of Indigenous and contemplative traditions, led him to this concept of the "intraconnected" Mwe and to the idea that people can change, grow, and grasp the importance of intraconnectedness.

His purpose with this book "is to explore the nature of our modern experience of separation, of the solo-self, and then consider pathways that offer the potential for large and lasting positive impacts on how we construct our sense of self, identity, and belonging that can help us in our individual, interpersonal and planetary lives as citizens on Earth. This is the mission of our journey" (p. 8).

Seigel presents findings from developmental science about how the self is created through personal, cultural, family, and religious teachings. He organizes that growth around chapters on the stages of human development—conception and womb life, toddlerhood, all along to maturity. Clearly, each human begins life in a womb totally connected to the mother. Events throughout our lives, and human neurobiology, demonstrate that we learn to separate from others as the body matures. That separation can be extreme or it can be mitigated by a broader understanding of the self's place in the cosmos. Within those chapters, he demonstrates how cultural evolution, too, is created in large communities and that they can move toward interconnectedness or separation. Thus, a person or a community can be taught—perhaps enlightened—about how to behave in an interconnected and intraconnected way rather than living as isolated and separate entities.

If we can grasp the magnitude of humanity's interconnectedness, and if we accept that the mind shapes each individual's identity, then it is possible to clear that solo-self illusion, Seigel asserts. And once that is accomplished, then the healing of the pandemics that face the Earth today can begin. He articulated six existing pandemics, those that affect all people and beings on the Earth because of our sense of separation (p. 7):

- COVID-19
- Social injustice focused on the dehumanization of out groups
- Environmental destruction
- Misinformation and polarization
- Attention addiction to comparison and competition, which causes a sense of inadequacy, inferiority, and incompleteness
- The cultural, or Western view, of an isolated, separate identity—or the solo-self

The book's concept in general can be conflated from Seigel's opening "Welcome" chapter:

> "A complex system is composed of interacting parts, often called nodes, and each node interacts with other nodes via their linkages. This is how the system functions. If a node functions as if it is the totally of its identity that it belongs only to its nodal part in the system, it will behave in a disconnected way, interdependence will shut down, and the whole complex system will lose its ability to adapt and learn. Its self-organization toward harmony will be compromised and instead the system will move toward chaos or rigidity. If the human mind has constructed a view of the self as separate, it may be that the body (a node) has come to identify itself as the whole self—rather than the self also including the whole of the systems in which that node (the body) exists. In medicine, when this happens to renegade cells in the body that grow without regard to the complex living somatic system, we call it cancer." (p. 5)

What exactly is the difference between interconnectedness and intraconnectedness? Those terms help connect the dots.

Interconnected suggests that there are things that interact—separate yet connected things. It is what Siegel calls a "betweenness" of something (p. 242). Recognizing these interconnections is essential to finding systems solutions to the pandemics facing the globe.

Intraconnection, on the other hand, encourages the understanding of the solo-self as actually the entire whole. "If a system is comprised of interacting elements, of nodes linked to one another, the solo-self perspective sees self as the node alone. What if a broader view—of the integrative whole self—shows that the self is the entirety of the system, revealing that in modern times we're mistaken the nodes for the whole source of self" (p. 240).

Thus, Me is actually We, and conflated to Mwe, that is the whole: what is going on in the self is the state of the cosmos. As above, so below, as within, so without.

As a scholar, Seigel brings together what science and philosophical traditions have been trying to teach I/Mwe/us for thousands and thousands of years. As he implied in the opening "Welcome," if you are willing to go on this journey of understanding, then we can move beyond the solo-self, even interconnectedness, to the place where intraconnectedness can become a reality.

Carol A. Atkinson, PhD, is a professor of digital media specializing in free speech, gender in the media, and personal interests in the myriad levels of consciousness. Email: Atkinson@retiree.ucmo.edu

The Burnout Antidote: A Spiritual Guide to Empowerment for Empaths, Over-Givers, and Highly Sensitive People

Anne Bérubé
Llewellyn, 2022
Softcover, 264 pages
$17.99
ISBN: 978-0738769738

Reviewed by Patricia Brancoforte

Empowerment is defined by the Merriam-Webster dictionary as: "1. The act or action of empowering someone or something; the granting of the power, right or authority to perform various acts or duties. 2. The state of being empowered to do something; the power, right or authority to do something."

Anne Bérubé fulfills the definition with her message that having empathy does not mean giving more than one has to give, leaving the highly sensitive feeling burnt out, but offers the means to connect to one's core essence, whereby a recharged energy and empowerment will emerge. Jumping right in from the beginning of *The Burnout Antidote*, she artfully maps out the intention of her book in the introduction, promising "a new way of engaging the spirit of service that is energizing, fulfilling and meaningful," thereby empowering rather than depleting those who serve.

Stating that burnout is the result of being of service even when it drains one's energy, thereby signaling that change is needed, she explains that serving should be inspired by the light within, not due to an external need. One can display the empathy necessary to understand others, but empaths need to do so without feeling the pain and suffering themselves. I feel her statement to "believe your body and what it's telling you" will resonate with each reader in his or her own way. How many times do we rationalize away a gut feeling only to regret it later?

By tapping into what she describes as our core essence, the author illustrates, through examples as well as meditation and journaling antidotes at the end of each chapter, the process by which the empath and highly sensitive individual is able to reclaim their power, while continuing to utilize their gift of service to others. Through her seven-step process, readers (even those inclined to overlook the antidote exercises) emerge with a positive perception of self, along with a renewed energy and sense of purpose. It should be noted that the meditations guide the newcomer to the practice while being familiar and comfortable for the seasoned practitioner.

The tools for transformation are defined clearly and concisely, beginning with the first chapter in which Bérubé states, "You are not responsible for the lives, wellbeing, happiness, or success of others…." Using examples, many from her own life experiences, she eloquently illustrates the properties of burnout, embodiment, core essence, and guilt, explaining how and why our soul may have chosen certain experiences and/or life paths, as well as the reemergence which can occur through the antidotes, using breathwork/mediation and journaling.

I was especially gratified by a single sentence in Chapter 5: "In time, you will find out who you really are, who you were before others needed you, before the world told you who you should be." I feel most, if not all, empaths, over-givers, and highly sensitive people will relate. Bérubé notes candidly that the transformative tools provided are not a quick fix, but rather an ongoing process to a healthier, more fulfilling, and energetic way of living.

The Burnout Antidote is a wonderful map for anyone wishing to connect with that core being, heal and understand past hurts, and live a more peaceful and contented life, while still being able to empathize and be of service to others.

Patricia Brancoforte is an author and artist who has also been a part of the metaphysical community for over 30 years, 20 of which were spent reading and teaching the Tarot. Email: pbrancoforte@outlook.com

Your Body Will Show You the Way: Energy Medicine for Personal and Global Change

Ellen Meredith

New World Library, 2022
Paperback, 360 pages
$19.95
ISBN: 978-1608688227

Reviewed by Dawn O'Creene

One question we have often heard is "How can we change the world?" Perhaps that answer lies within these pages. Ellen Meredith believes that we start with ourselves. As each body of water is made up of infinite droplets, the totality of humanity is comprised of each individual being. The soul of each individual has its own energy field that feeds into the whole of a greater energy field. Doing the work at ground zero can transform your own life and that higher energy, in turn, flows into the collective energy field.

Meredith is an energy healer and medical intuitive, having studied under one of the renowned energy healers and teachers, Donna Eden. She has also been trained by her inner teachers whom she calls her "Councils." The goal of *Your Body Will Show You the Way* is to help navigate radical change, assist in moving from chaos to clarity, and help guide from illness to wellness in all of its forms. Within these pages, you will find a vast collection of energetic journeys that can be experienced in their entirety or as one's energy and needs dictate.

In these pages, you will learn the Six Dynamics of Wellbeing:

- Gatekeeping
- Grounding
- Coherence
- Flow
- Exchange Between Oneself and the World
- Radiance

Meredith believes that the world has been living in an "Outside In" (Yang) state. We rely on the "experts" to tell us who we are and what we need to do. She encourages us to move to a more balanced "Inside Out" (Yin) state in order to find our true natures and help heal ourselves in a more organic way, thus finding our answers from within.

This involves learning to speak more fluently in a dialogue with the various energies of your body. Meredith believes that we each have a Gatekeeper, which is like an all-encompassing immune system composed of our physical, mental, emotional, and spiritual systems. It is also quite protective and a bit like a helicopter mom. The Gatekeeper's job is safety in all respects. It is there also to build and protect your identity, maintain habits, and allocate energies to the priorities of the inner selves. Befriending and partnering with your Gatekeeper is essential. That will often be the starting point of getting to the root of any issue. When the Gatekeeper is triggered, a person generally feels unsafe, has polarized thinking, and is very reactive. Fear not, there is plenty here to help bring the energy out of chaos.

Meredith notes that there are three skill sets that will help you reclaim your inner guidance: Learning to sense subtle energies; learning to locate the issue, or who (in your body) needs to communicate now; and learning to work energetically with what you discover. Through these skill sets, you can learn how to dialogue with your many different selves.

While some of the practices are longer, some are more concise and can change your energies immediately. There is a wonderful list of practices to try "While Stuck Waiting." In our world of lines, traffic, and hold music, we have many opportunities to employ one of these. Porcupine Reset and Pet the Doggie/Kitty are designed for when one is in the middle of an energetic crisis and aim at calming the Gatekeeper.

We can't always avoid being triggered and Meredith offers practices to get back into balance. Like a yard that has been littered with debris after a storm, our energy needs cleaning up post storm to remove stress hormones that cause a flood of undesirable consequences. She offers the Energy Relay Reset and Gatekeeper Syncing, which helps reset the Yin communication. The wonderful part is that the Gatekeeper actually wants to work with you. Anything you do to befriend it helps reinstate a healthy balance and flow.

While Meredith does incorporate the chakras into the work, she wants you to put aside the standard chakra lore for now and see it from another angle: chakras as doorways into your own energetic storehouses of experience. They can assist you in changing your inner landscape and how you are treated in the world. There are some innovative exercises for these, including Fishing in the Chakras. I was inspired to take her idea of cleaning the chakra "vents" and created my own practice with it, because after all, these practices are all geared to what your own intuitions are telling you.

Entering Streams is an incredibly important option in working with your inner energies. You can drop into the appropriate meridian to perceive, interact, and ask, "What do you need?" You can be open to new perspectives and energy guidance and thereby bring support to where the energies live. This can be done via the Guided Visit practice. These visits, among other benefits, can help you:

- Explore and discover
- Repair or renovate
- Plant seeds of change
- Make pacts with the guides or with yourself there
- Ask for guidance/seek visions

These visits will help you create direct relationships with the spaces you visit, which results in stronger understanding and intuitions that will ultimately assist in creating an inner landscape of your choosing.

Illuminated here is the point that we need to take the time to do the work and find out what we need through energetic and emotional self-examination. Exploring our inner energy systems involves going within these streams. The exercises offered can help you do that, guiding you in learning more of who you are by identifying what feeds you and also what repels you. In the process, you become the expert on you and cultivate more of the Inside Out atmosphere.

The practices in this book are playful and imaginative, with varying levels of time needed to do them. They can help you shape your life in numerous ways, including increasing your radiance. When we all pass along our genuine radiance to others and into the greater energy field, we just may be in the process of changing the world.

Dawn O'Creene works as a finance analyst by day and enjoys being a library clerk by night. You can find her on the stage of her community theater when she is not working behind the scenes. She believes you can never stop learning or have too many books. Email: gazingraven@gmail.com

The Energy to Heal: Find Lasting Freedom from Stress and Trauma Through Energy Medicine Yoga

Lauren Walker

Llewellyn, 2022
Softcover, 224 pages
$17.99
ISBN: 978-0738769493

Reviewed by Carol A. Atkinson

The yoga maxim "The mind may forget, but the body always remembers" is the key to Lauren Walker's book *The Energy to Heal.* The concept of energy medicine yoga emerged from the pain of her own trauma, as she used the myriad energy systems, asanas, breathing, and the five elements to calm her own energy bodies and to help her physical body release and forget the pain of her experience.

Walker admits to a personal relationship that ended so badly—that friend was eventually killed by law enforcement after a manhunt—she was thrown into a depression from which she could not emerge. After a year, she found her way back through the use of yoga, developing a practice she called Energy Medicine Yoga. The practice includes working with nine energy systems (pp. 18–19):

- The Aura: The first system to appear around a cell at conception, it is the blueprint of any entity.
- Electrics: connects all the other systems together and is the rhythm of the Earth's energy
- Radiant Circuits: the energies of joy and healing, arising naturally from the pulsing of the electrics
- Chakras: As a person grows, he or she accrues information that soon becomes spinning vortexes of energy; these are the energetic hard drive.
- Meridians: Emerging from the repetitive movement of the radiant circuits as lines of energy, meridians are grooved pathways that link the organs together in one continuous line of energy.
- Triple Warmer: This runs the immune system and was once a radiant circuit and a meridian; now it conserves the "Self" against the "other."
- Five elements: The earth rhythm first to emerge in the electrics spreads out and aligns the emerging body with the five elements (water, wood, fire, earth, and metal).
- The Grid: the deepest energy system and that to which the other energy systems anchor
- The Celtic Weave: The outermost layer of the aura, it weaves all the energies of the body together.

Walker's Energy Medicine Yoga is a system organized around the five elements using journaling, extensive asanas, breathing, and energy practices that help open and release stuck energy in these nine systems. She helps the reader "see" the organization of the five elements through the five-pointed star of traditional Chinese medicine (TCM):

> "You will learn how to hold the…[s]tar up to an experience and see which point of the star is stuck, frozen, and darkened by the trauma; which part of your inner light has been snuffed out. Once you know that, you'll work within the particular element (or two) to learn how to relight that point. You want every point of the star to be open and flowing with energy. Each point is a shining light." (p. 26)

The sum of these practices could be viewed as a prescription for an identified trauma. A practitioner can move through the five-pointed star to work generally with each element, or perhaps to identity the primary emotional aspect of the trauma. At that point, the practitioner can match that to the core of each element, asking, for example (p. 37):

- What am I afraid of here? Where is my courage? Am I stuck in fear? Then work on the journaling, breathing, and asanas found in the chapter on the water element titled "Raise Your Courage with Water."
- What am I still angry about? Is there any action I could take to help resolve this? Am I stuck in anger? Then move to the wood element chapter titled "Speak Your Truth with Wood."
- What makes me anxious about this situation? Can I get some inspiration on how to move forward? Am I stuck in anxiety? Then move to the fire element chapter titled "Transform with Fire."
- Why am I so worried about *everyone* else in this situation? What am *I* actually feeling about this? Am I stuck in worry? Then move to the earth element chapter titled "Learn to Love Again with Earth."
- What is the saddest part of this? Am I ready to let it go? Am I stuck in grief? Then go to the metal chapter titled "Find Faith with Metal."

Walker also provides a quiz for readers to identify their own personal primary and secondary elements, elements that are theirs for life. This process can help clear out any stuckness or, more important, help readers understand how they deal with illnesses or emotional upsets in their own bodies.

Walker reminds the reader that as each person heals themselves, they heal others. "Your healing—the shifting of your energy—affects every person you come into contact with. And their shift in energy continues to radiate out" (p. 191). As trauma and anger are released, the person becomes kinder and gentler to themselves and to others. "Heal yourself, heal the world," she wrote (p. 191).

Energy Medicine Yoga is an interesting mix of using the emotional body to guide the work, then using the mental body to sort out the beliefs or feelings, and then when one or more emotional blockages are brought into consciousness, they can be sweetly released through the gentleness of yoga and energy medicine. While there is an overall bit of sadness to the book (perhaps from the unfolding story of her friend who died), it is a compelling read and well worth doing the work to which Walker gives us access. It is wonderful that she provided this content outside of her physical yoga studio.

Carol A. Atkinson, PhD, is a professor of digital media specializing in free speech, gender in the media, and personal interests in the myriad levels of consciousness. Email: Atkinson@retiree.ucmo.edu

AGING

Probabilistic forecasting of maximum human lifespan by 2100 using Bayesian population projections

Pearce, M., & Raftery, A. E. (2021). Probabilistic forecasting of maximum human lifespan by 2100 using Bayesian population projections. *Demographic Research, 44*, 1271–1294. doi:10.4054/DemRes.2021.44.52

Abstract

Background: We consider the problem of quantifying the human lifespan using a statistical approach that probabilistically forecasts the maximum reported age at death (MRAD) through 2100.

Objective: We seek to quantify the probability that any person attains various extreme ages, such as those above 120, by the year 2100.

Methods: We use the exponential survival model for supercentenarians (people over age 110) of Rootzén and Zholud (2017) but extend the forecasting window, quantify population uncertainty using Bayesian population projections, and incorporate the most recent data from the International Database on Longevity (IDL) to obtain unconditional estimates of the distribution of MRAD this century in a fully Bayesian analysis.

Results: We find that the exponential survival model for supercentenarians is consistent with the most recent IDL data and that projections of the population aged 110–114 through 2080 are sensible. We integrate over the posterior distributions of the exponential model parameter and uncertainty in the supercentenarian population projections to estimate an unconditional distribution of MRAD by 2100.

Conclusions: Based on the Bayesian analysis, there is a greater than 99% probability that the current MRAD of 122 will be broken by 2100. We estimate the probabilities that a person lives to at least age 126, 128, or 130 this century, as 89%, 44%, and 13%, respectively.

Diploid hepatocytes drive physiological liver renewal in adult humans

Heinke, P., Rost, F., Rode, J., Trus, P., Simonova, I., Lázár, E., … Bergmann, O. (2022). Diploid hepatocytes drive physiological liver renewal in adult humans. *Cell Systems, 13*(6), 499–507. doi:10.1016/j.cels.2022.05.001

Abstract

Physiological liver cell replacement is central to maintaining the organ's high metabolic activity, although its characteristics are difficult to study in humans. Using retrospective radiocarbon (^{14}C) birth dating of cells, we report that human hepatocytes show continuous and lifelong turnover, allowing the liver to remain a young organ (average age < 3 years). Hepatocyte renewal is highly dependent on the ploidy level. Diploid hepatocytes show more than 7-fold higher annual birth rates than polyploid hepatocytes. These observations support the view that physiological liver cell renewal in humans is mainly dependent on diploid hepatocytes, whereas polyploid cells are compromised in their ability to divide. Moreover, cellular transitions between diploid and polyploid hepatocytes are limited under homeostatic conditions. With these findings, we present an integrated model of homeostatic liver cell generation in humans that provides fundamental insights into liver cell turnover dynamics.

ANXIETY/DEPRESSION

Individual and work factors associated with psychosocial health of registered nurses during the Covid-19 pandemic: A mixed methods study

Witkoski Stimpfel, A., Ghazal, L., Goldsamt, L., & Vaughan Dickson, V. (2022). Individual and work factors associated with psychosocial health of registered nurses during the Covid-19 pandemic: A mixed methods study. *Journal of Occupational and Environmental Medicine*, *64*(6), 515–524. doi:10.1097/JOM.0000000000002495

Abstract

Objective: To describe the initial influence of the Covid-19 pandemic on U.S. nurses' psychosocial health, and to identify factors associated with poor psychosocial health outcomes.

Methods: We conducted a convergent (QUAN+qual) mixed methods study. From June to August 2020, we administered surveys ($N = 629$) and conducted semi-structured interviews ($N = 34$) among nurses working across healthcare settings in 18 states. We developed separate multivariable logistic regression models for three psychosocial outcomes (anxiety, depressive symptoms, insomnia). We used content analysis to process and analyze qualitative data, and integrated results in the final analysis step.

Results: Nurses reported high rates of depressive symptoms (22%), anxiety (52%), and insomnia (55%). Disturbances to sleep were both a contributing factor to, and an outcome of, poor psychosocial health.

Conclusions: Evidence-based interventions addressing work stress and sleep, and proactive monitoring of nurses' psychosocial health by employers are urgently needed.

Mindfulness-based stress reduction vs escitalopram for the treatment of adults with anxiety disorders: A randomized clinical trial

Hoge, E. A., Bui, E., Mete, M., Dutton, M. A., Baker, A. W., & Simon, N. M. (2023). Mindfulness-based stress reduction vs escitalopram for the treatment of adults with anxiety disorders: A randomized clinical trial. *JAMA Psychiatry*, *80*(1), 13–21. doi:10.1001/jamapsychiatry.2022.3679

Abstract

Importance: Anxiety disorders are common, highly distressing, and impairing conditions. Effective treatments exist, but many patients do not access or respond to them. Mindfulness-based interventions, such as mindfulness-based stress reduction (MBSR) are popular and can decrease anxiety, but it is unknown how they compare to standard first-line treatments.

Objective: To determine whether MBSR is noninferior to escitalopram, a commonly used first-line psychopharmacological treatment for anxiety disorders.

Design, setting, and participants: This randomized clinical trial (Treatments for Anxiety: Meditation and Escitalopram [TAME]) included a noninferiority design with a prespecified noninferiority margin. Patients were recruited between June 2018 and February 2020. The outcome assessments were performed by blinded clinical interviewer at baseline, week 8 end point, and follow-up visits at 12 and 24 weeks. Of 430 individuals assessed for inclusion, 276 adults with a diagnosed anxiety disorder from three urban academic medical centers in the US were recruited for the trial, and 208 completed the trial.

Interventions: Participants were 1:1 randomized to 8 weeks of the weekly MBSR course or the antidepressant escitalopram, flexibly dosed from 10 to 20 mg.

Main outcomes and measures: The primary outcome measure was anxiety levels as assessed with the Clinical Global Impression of Severity scale (CGI-S), with a predetermined noninferiority margin of –0.495 points.

Results: The primary noninferiority sample consisted of 208 patients (102 in MBSR and 106 in escitalopram), with a mean (SD) age of 33 (13) years; 156 participants (75%) were female; 32 participants (15%) were African American, 41 (20%) were Asian, 18 (9%) were Hispanic/Latino, 122 (59%) were White, and 13 (6%) were of another race or ethnicity (including Native American or Alaska Native, more than one race, or other, consolidated owing to low numbers). Baseline mean (SD) CGI-S score was 4.44 (0.79) for the MBSR group and 4.51 (0.78) for the escitalopram group in the per-protocol sample and 4.49 (0.77) vs 4.54 (0.83), respectively, in the randomized sample. At end point, the mean (SD) CGI-S score was reduced by 1.35 (1.06) for MBSR and 1.43 (1.17) for escitalopram. The difference between groups was –0.07 (0.16; 95% CI, –0.38 to 0.23; $p = .65$), where the lower bound of the interval fell within the predefined noninferiority margin of –0.495, indicating noninferiority of MBSR compared with escitalopram. Secondary intent-to-treat analyses using imputed data also showed the noninferiority of MBSR compared with escitalopram based on the improvement in CGI-S score. Of patients who started treatment, 10 (8%) dropped out of the escitalopram group and none from the MBSR group due to adverse events. At least one study-related adverse event occurred for 110 participants randomized to escitalopram (78.6%) and 21 participants randomized to MBSR (15.4%).

Conclusions and relevance: The results from this randomized clinical trial comparing a standardized evidence-based mindfulness-based intervention with pharmacotherapy for the treatment of anxiety disorders found that MBSR was noninferior to escitalopram.

Night owls and lone wolves

Norbury, R. (2022). Night owls and lone wolves. *Biological Rhythm Research, 53*(11), 1702–1710. doi:10.1080/09291016.2021.2014083

Abstract

Diurnal preference for evening time has been associated with poorer physical and mental health outcomes. In the current report, perceived loneliness and brain structure (hippocampal and amygdala volumes) were compared in a large ($N = 4684$) sample of morning- and evening-type individuals. Definite eveningness was associated with increased odds for reporting self-perceived loneliness, and lonely evening types had significantly smaller right hippocampal volume as compared to morning and more socially connected evening types. These data add to the mounting body of evidence linking an evening profile with increased risk for psychiatric disorder.

Depression alters the circadian pattern of online activity

Ten Thij, M., Bathina, K., Rutter, L. A., Lorenzo-Luaces, L., van de Leemput, I. A., Scheffer, M., & Bollen, J. (2020). Depression alters the circadian pattern of online activity. *Scientific Reports*, *10*(1), 1–10. doi:10.1038/s41598-020-74314-3

Abstract

Human sleep/wake cycles follow a stable circadian rhythm associated with hormonal, emotional, and cognitive changes. Changes of this cycle are implicated in many mental health concerns. In fact, the bidirectional relation between major depressive disorder and sleep has been well documented. Despite a clear link between sleep disturbances and subsequent disturbances in mood, it is difficult to determine from self-reported data which specific changes of the sleep/wake cycle play the most important role in this association. Here we observe marked changes of activity cycles in millions of Twitter posts of 688 subjects who explicitly stated in unequivocal terms that they had received a (clinical) diagnosis of depression as compared to the activity cycles of a large control group ($n = 8791$). Rather than a phase-shift, as reported in other work, we find significant changes of activity levels in the evening and before dawn. Compared to the control group, depressed subjects were significantly more active from 7 PM to midnight and less active from 3 to 6 AM. Content analysis of tweets revealed a steady rise in rumination and emotional content from midnight to dawn among depressed individuals. These results suggest that diagnosis and treatment of depression may focus on modifying the timing of activity, reducing rumination, and decreasing social media use at specific hours of the day.

Watching the world from my screen: A longitudinal evaluation of the influence of a problematic use of the internet on depressive symptomatology

Hernandez, C., Cottin, M., Parada, F., Labbe, N., Nunez, C., Quevedo, Y., … Behn, A. (2022). Watching the world from my screen: A longitudinal evaluation of the influence of a problematic use of the internet on depressive symptomatology. *Computers in Human Behavior*, *126*, 106995. doi:10.1016/j.chb.2021.106995

Abstract

Previous research has found a consistent association between depressive symptomatology and a problematic use of the internet, however, the causal pathways responsible for this association are not well known. Following emotion regulation theory, the present study aimed to explore the longitudinal dynamics between using the internet to distract oneself, difficulties controlling internet use, and depressive symptoms. A sample of 163 adults from Chile completed intensive self-reports about internet use and depressive symptoms over 35 days. Using growth curve models, we predicted depressive symptoms both by a person's average tendency (between-subjects) to use the internet for distraction and having problems controlling internet use, and by momentary fluctuations (within-subjects). We also tested a model with reversed paths. Results indicate that momentary increases in distraction are not associated with depressive symptoms, however, increases in the latter were associated with more distraction. The relationship between distraction and depressive symptoms was mediated by difficulties controlling internet use, but only at the between-subjects level. This suggests that a higher average tendency to use the internet to distract oneself may work as an emotional buffer, with negative emotional consequences in the long run, an effect that takes time to completely unfold. Theoretical and practical implications are discussed.

Physical activity reduces clinical symptoms and restores neuroplasticity in major depression

Brüchle, W., Schwarzer, C., Berns, C., Scho, S., Schneefeld, J., Koester, D., … Rosenkranz, K. (2021). Physical activity reduces clinical symptoms and restores neuroplasticity in major depression. *Frontiers in Psychiatry, 935.* doi:10.3389/fpsyt.2021.660642

Abstract

Major depressive disorder (MDD) is the most common mental disorder and deficits in neuroplasticity are discussed as one pathophysiological mechanism. Physical activity (PA) enhances neuroplasticity in healthy subjects and improves clinical symptoms of MDD. However, it is unclear whether this clinical effect of PA is due to restoring deficient neuroplasticity in MDD. We investigated the effect of a 3-week PA program applied on clinical symptoms, motor excitability and plasticity, and on cognition in patients with MDD ($n = 23$), in comparison to a control intervention (CI; $n = 18$). Before and after the interventions, the clinical symptom severity was tested using self- (BDI-II) and investigator- (HAMD-17) rated scales, transcranial magnetic stimulation (TMS) protocols were used to test motor excitability and paired-associative stimulation (PAS) to test long-term-potentiation (LTP)–like plasticity. Additionally, cognitive functions such as attention, working memory and executive functions were tested. After the interventions, the BDI-II and HAMD-17 decreased significantly in both groups, but the decrease in HAMD-17 was significantly stronger in the PA group. Cognition did not change notably in either group. Motor excitability did not differ between the groups and remained unchanged by either intervention. Baseline levels of LTP-like plasticity in the motor cortex were low in both groups (PA: 113.40 ± 2.55%; CI: 116.83 ± 3.70%) and increased significantly after PA (155.06 ± 10.48%) but not after CI (122.01 ± 4.1%). Higher baseline BDI-II scores were correlated with lower levels of neuroplasticity. Importantly, the more the BDI-II score decreased during the interventions, the stronger did neuroplasticity increase. The latter effect was particularly strong after PA ($r = -0.835$; $p < 0.001$). The level of neuroplasticity related specifically to the psychological/affective items, which are tested predominantly in the BDI-II. However, the significant clinical difference in the intervention effects was shown in the HAMD-17 which focuses more on somatic/neurovegetative items known to improve earlier in the course of MDD. In summary, PA improved symptoms of MDD and restored the deficient neuroplasticity. Importantly, both changes were strongly related on the individual patient's level, highlighting the key role of neuroplasticity in the pathophysiology and the clinical relevance of neuroplasticity-enhancing interventions for the treatment of MDD.

Frequent interpersonal stress and inflammatory reactivity predict depressive-symptom increases: Two tests of the social-signal-transduction theory of depression

Madison, A. A., Andridge, R., Shrout, M. R., Renna, M. E., Bennett, J. M., Jaremka, L. M., ... Kiecolt-Glaser, J. K. (2022). Frequent interpersonal stress and inflammatory reactivity predict depressive-symptom increases: Two tests of the social-signal-transduction theory of depression. *Psychological Science*, *33*(1), 152–164. doi:10.1177/09567976211031225

Abstract

The social-signal-transduction theory of depression asserts that people who experience ongoing interpersonal stressors and mount a greater inflammatory response to social stress are at higher risk for depression. The current study tested this theory in two adult samples. In Study 1, physically healthy adults ($N = 76$) who reported more frequent interpersonal tension had heightened depressive symptoms at Visit 2, but only if they had greater inflammatory reactivity to a marital conflict at Visit 1. Similarly, in Study 2, depressive symptoms increased among lonelier and less socially supported breast-cancer survivors ($N = 79$). This effect was most pronounced among participants with higher inflammatory reactivity to a social-evaluative stressor at Visit 1. In both studies, non-interpersonal stress did not interact with inflammatory reactivity to predict later depressive symptoms.

Single-dose psilocybin for a treatment-resistant episode of major depression

Goodwin, G. M., Aaronson, S. T., Alvarez, O., Arden, P. C., Baker, A., Bennett, J. C., ... Malievskaia, E. (2022). Single-dose psilocybin for a treatment-resistant episode of major depression. *New England Journal of Medicine*, *387*(18), 1637–1648. doi:10.1056/NEJMoa2206443

Abstract

Background: Psilocybin is being studied for use in treatment-resistant depression.

Methods: In this phase 2 double-blind trial, we randomly assigned adults with treatment-resistant depression to receive a single dose of a proprietary, synthetic formulation of psilocybin at a dose of 25 mg, 10 mg, or 1 mg (control), along with psychological support. The primary end point was the change from baseline to week 3 in the total score on the Montgomery-Åsberg Depression Rating Scale (MADRS; range, 0 to 60, with higher scores indicating more severe depression). Secondary end points included response at week 3 (≥50% decrease from baseline in the MADRS total score), remission at week 3 (MADRS total score ≤ 10), and sustained response at 12 weeks (meeting response criteria at week 3 and all subsequent visits).

Results: A total of 79 participants were in the 25-mg group, 75 in the 10-mg group, and 79 in the 1-mg group. The mean MADRS total score at baseline was 32 or 33 in each group. Least-squares mean changes from baseline to week 3 in the score were –12.0 for 25 mg, –7.9 for 10 mg, and –5.4 for 1 mg; the difference between the 25-mg group and 1-mg group was –6.6 (95% confidence interval [CI], –10.2 to –2.9; $p < 0.001$) and between the 10-mg group and 1-mg group was –2.5 (95% CI, –6.2 to 1.2; $p = 0.18$). In the 25-mg group, the incidences of response and remission at 3 weeks, but not sustained response at 12 weeks, were generally supportive of the primary results. Adverse events occurred in 179 of 233 participants (77%) and included headache, nausea, and dizziness. Suicidal ideation or behavior or self-injury occurred in all dose groups.

Conclusions: In this phase 2 trial involving participants with treatment-resistant depression, psilocybin at a single dose of 25 mg, but not 10 mg, reduced depression scores significantly more than a 1-mg dose over a period of 3 weeks but was associated with adverse effects. Larger and longer trials, including comparison with existing treatments, are required to determine the efficacy and safety of psilocybin for this disorder.

Molecular mechanisms of psilocybin and implications for the treatment of depression

Ling, S., Ceban, F., Lui, L. M., Lee, Y., Teopiz, K. M., Rodrigues, N. B., ... McIntyre, R. S. (2022). Molecular mechanisms of psilocybin and implications for the treatment of depression. *CNS Drugs*, *36*(1), 17–30. doi:10.1007/s40263-021-00877-y

Abstract

Therapeutic deficiencies with monoaminergic antidepressants invite the need to identify and develop novel rapid-acting antidepressants. Hitherto, ketamine and esketamine are identified as safe, well-tolerated rapid-acting antidepressants in adults with treatment-resistant depression, and also mitigate measures of suicidality. Psilocybin is a naturally occurring psychoactive alkaloid and non-selective agonist at many serotonin receptors, especially at serotonin 5-HT_{2A} receptors, and is found in the *Psilocybe* genus of mushrooms. Preliminary studies with psilocybin have shown therapeutic promise across diverse populations including major depressive disorder. The pharmacodynamic mechanisms mediating the antidepressant and psychedelic effects of psilocybin are currently unknown but are thought to involve the modulation of the serotonergic system, primarily through agonism at the 5-HT_{2A} receptors and downstream changes in gene expression. It is also established that indirect effects on dopaminergic and glutamatergic systems are contributory, as well as effects at other lower affinity targets. Along with the direct effects on neurochemical systems, psilocybin alters neural circuitry and key brain regions previously implicated in depression, including the default mode network and amygdala. The aim of this review is to synthesize the current understanding of the receptor pharmacology and neuronal mechanisms underlying the psychedelic and putative antidepressant properties of psilocybin.

ATTITUDES/BELIEFS

Can behavioral interventions be too salient? Evidence from traffic safety messages

Hall, J. D., & Madsen, J. M. (2022). Can behavioral interventions be too salient? Evidence from traffic safety messages. *Science*, *376*(6591), eabm3427. doi:10.1126/science.abm3427

Abstract

Although behavioral interventions are designed to seize attention, little consideration has been given to the costs of doing so. We estimated these costs in the context of a safety campaign that, to encourage safe driving, displays traffic fatality counts on highway dynamic message signs for one week each month. We found that crashes increase statewide during campaign weeks, which is inconsistent with any benefits. Furthermore, these effects do not persist beyond campaign weeks. Our results show that behavioral interventions, particularly negatively framed ones, can be too salient, crowding out more important considerations and causing interventions to backfire-with costly consequences.

People mistake the internet's knowledge for their own

Ward, A. F. (2021). People mistake the internet's knowledge for their own. *Proceedings of the National Academy of Sciences*, *118*(43), e2105061118. doi:10.1073/pnas.2105061118

Abstract

People frequently search the internet for information. Eight experiments (n = 1,917) provide evidence that when people "Google" for online information, they fail to distinguish accurately between knowledge stored internally (in their own memories) and knowledge stored externally (on the internet). Relative to those using only their own knowledge, people who use Google to answer general knowledge questions are not only more confident in their ability to access external information; they are also more confident in their own ability to think and remember. Moreover, those who use Google predict that they will know more in the future without the help of the internet, an erroneous belief that both indicates misattribution of prior knowledge and highlights a practically important consequence of this misattribution: overconfidence when the internet is no longer available. Although humans have long relied on external knowledge, the misattribution of online knowledge to the self may be facilitated by the swift and seamless interface between internal thought and external information that characterizes online search. Online search is often faster than internal memory search, preventing people from fully recognizing the limitations of their own knowledge. The internet delivers information seamlessly, dovetailing with internal cognitive processes and offering minimal physical cues that might draw attention to its contributions. As a result, people may lose sight of where their own knowledge ends and where the internet's knowledge begins. Thinking with Google may cause people to mistake the internet's knowledge for their own.

Overly shallow?: Miscalibrated expectations create a barrier to deeper conversation

Kardas, M., Kumar, A., & Epley, N. (2022). Overly shallow?: Miscalibrated expectations create a barrier to deeper conversation. *Journal of Personality and Social Psychology, 122*(3), 367. doi:10.1037/pspa0000281

Abstract

People may want deep and meaningful relationships with others, but may also be reluctant to engage in the deep and meaningful conversations with strangers that could create those relationships. We hypothesized that people systematically underestimate how caring and interested distant strangers are in one's own intimate revelations and that these miscalibrated expectations create a psychological barrier to deeper conversations. As predicted, conversations between strangers felt less awkward, and created more connectedness and happiness, than the participants themselves expected (Experiments 1a–5). Participants were especially prone to overestimate how awkward deep conversations would be compared with shallow conversations (Experiments 2–5). Notably, they also felt more connected to deep conversation partners than shallow conversation partners after having both types of conversations (Experiments 6a–b). Systematic differences between expectations and experiences arose because participants expected others to care less about their disclosures in conversation than others actually did (Experiments 1a, 1b, 4a, 4b, 5, and 6a). As a result, participants more accurately predicted the outcomes of their conversations when speaking with close friends, family, or partners whose care and interest are more clearly known (Experiment 5). Miscalibrated expectations about others matter because they guide decisions about which topics to discuss in conversation, such that more calibrated expectations encourage deeper conversation (Experiments 7a–7b). Misunderstanding others can encourage overly shallow interactions.

The Einstein effect provides global evidence for scientific source credibility effects and the influence of religiosity

Hoogeveen, S., Haaf, J. M., Bulbulia, J. A., Ross, R. M., McKay, R., Altay, S., … van Elk, M. (2022). The Einstein effect provides global evidence for scientific source credibility effects and the influence of religiosity. *Nature Human Behaviour, 6*(4), 523–535. doi:10.1038/s41562-021-01273-8

Abstract

People tend to evaluate information from reliable sources more favorably, but it is unclear exactly how perceivers' worldviews interact with this source credibility effect. In a large and diverse cross-cultural sample (N = 10,195 from 24 countries), we presented participants with obscure, meaningless statements attributed to either a spiritual guru or a scientist. We found a robust global source credibility effect for scientific authorities, which we dub "the Einstein effect": across all 24 countries and all levels of religiosity, scientists held greater authority than spiritual gurus. In addition, individual religiosity predicted a weaker relative preference for the statement from the scientist compared with the spiritual guru, and was more strongly associated with credibility judgments for the guru than the scientist. Independent data on explicit trust ratings across 143 countries mirrored our experimental findings. These findings suggest that irrespective of one's religious worldview, across cultures science is a powerful and universal heuristic that signals the reliability of information.

Knowledge overconfidence is associated with anti-consensus views on controversial scientific issues

Light, N., Fernbach, P. M., Rabb, N., Geana, M. V., & Sloman, S. A. (2022). Knowledge overconfidence is associated with anti-consensus views on controversial scientific issues. *Science Advances*, *8*(29), eabo0038. doi:10.1126/sciadv.abo0038

Abstract
Public attitudes that are in opposition to scientific consensus can be disastrous and include rejection of vaccines and opposition to climate change mitigation policies. Five studies examine the interrelationships between opposition to expert consensus on controversial scientific issues, how much people actually know about these issues, and how much they think they know. Across seven critical issues that enjoy substantial scientific consensus, as well as attitudes toward COVID-19 vaccines and mitigation measures like mask wearing and social distancing, results indicate that those with the highest levels of opposition have the lowest levels of objective knowledge but the highest levels of subjective knowledge. Implications for scientists, policymakers, and science communicators are discussed.

"Just letting you know ... " Underestimating others' desire for constructive feedback

Abi-Esber, N., Abel, J. E., Schroeder, J., & Gino, F. (2022). "Just letting you know..." Underestimating others' desire for constructive feedback. *Journal of Personality and Social Psychology, 123*(6), 1362–1385. doi:10.1037/pspi0000393

Abstract
People sometimes avoid giving feedback to others even when it would help fix others' problems. For example, only 2.6% of individuals in a pilot field study provided feedback to a survey administrator who had food or lipstick on their face. Five experiments (N = 1,984) identify a possible reason for the lack of feedback: People underestimate how much others want to receive constructive feedback. Initial experiments demonstrated this underestimation of others' desire for feedback in hypothetical scenarios (Experiment 1), recalled feedback experiences (Experiment 2), and real-time feedback among friends (Experiment 3). We further examine how people ascertain others' desire for feedback, testing how much they consider the potential consequences of feedback for themselves (e.g., discomfort giving feedback or harm to their relationship with the receiver) or the receiver (e.g., discomfort receiving feedback or value from feedback). While we found evidence that people consider both types of consequences, people particularly underestimated how much receivers value their feedback, a mechanism not extensively tested in prior research. Specifically, in Experiment 4, two interventions-making feedback-givers consider receivers' perspectives (enhancing consideration of receivers' consequences) or imagine someone else providing feedback (reducing consideration of givers' consequences) both improved givers' recognition of others' desire for feedback compared to no intervention, but the perspective-taking intervention was most effective. Finally, Experiment 5 demonstrates the underestimation during a financially incentivized public-speaking contest and shows that giving less constructive feedback resulted in less improvement in feedback-receivers' performances. Overall, people consistently underestimate others' desire for feedback, with potentially negative consequences for feedback-receivers' outcomes.

BRAIN/COGNITION

Functional connectivity signatures of political ideology

Yang, S. E., Wilson, J. D., Lu, Z. L., & Cranmer, S. (2022). Functional connectivity signatures of political ideology. *PNAS Nexus*, *1*(3), pgac066. doi:10.1093/pnasnexus/pgac066

Abstract
Emerging research has begun investigating the neural underpinnings of the biological and psychological differences that drive political ideology, attitudes, and actions. Here, we explore the neurological roots of politics through conducting a large sample, whole-brain analysis of functional connectivity (FC) across common fMRI tasks. Using convolutional neural networks, we develop predictive models of ideology using FC from fMRI scans for nine standard task-based settings in a novel cohort of healthy adults (n = 174, age range: 18 to 40, mean = 21.43) from the

Ohio State University Wellbeing Project. Our analyses suggest that liberals and conservatives have noticeable and discriminative differences in FC that can be identified with high accuracy using contemporary artificial intelligence methods and that such analyses complement contemporary models relying on socioeconomic and survey-based responses. FC signatures from retrieval, empathy, and monetary reward tasks are identified as important and powerful predictors of conservatism, and activations of the amygdala, inferior frontal gyrus, and hippocampus are most strongly associated with political affiliation. Although the direction of causality is unclear, this study suggests that the biological and neurological roots of political behavior run much deeper than previously thought.

Threat history controls flexible escape behavior in mice

Lenzi, S. C., Cossell, L., Grainger, B., Olesen, S. F., Branco, T., & Margrie, T. W. (2022). Threat history controls flexible escape behavior in mice. *Current Biology*, *32*(13), 2972–2979. doi:10.1016/j.cub.2022.05.022

Abstract

In many instances, external sensory-evoked neuronal activity is used by the brain to select the most appropriate behavioral response. Predator-avoidance behaviors such as freezing and escape are of particular interest since these stimulus-evoked responses are behavioral manifestations of a decision-making process that is fundamental to survival. Over the lifespan of an individual, however, the threat value of agents in the environment is believed to undergo constant revision, and in some cases, repeated avoidance of certain stimuli may no longer be an optimal behavioral strategy. To begin to study this type of adaptive control of decision-making, we devised an experimental paradigm to probe the properties of threat escape in the laboratory mouse *Mus musculus*. First, we found that while robust escape to visual looming stimuli can be observed after two days of social isolation, mice can also rapidly learn that such stimuli are non-threatening. This learned suppression of escape (LSE) is extremely robust and can persist for weeks and is not a generalized adaptation, since flight responses to novel live prey and auditory threat stimuli in the same environmental context were maintained. We also show that LSE cannot be explained by trial number or a simple form of stimulus desensitization since it is dependent on threat-escape history. We propose that the action selection process mediating escape behavior is constantly updated by recent threat history and that LSE can be used as a robust model system to understand the neurophysiological mechanisms underlying experience-dependent decision-making.

Oxytocin and vasotocin receptor variation and the evolution of human prosociality

Theofanopoulou, C., Andirkó, A., Boeckx, C., & Jarvis, E. D. (2022). Oxytocin and vasotocin receptor variation and the evolution of human prosociality. *Comprehensive Psychoneuroendocrinology*, *11*, 100139. doi:10.1016/j.cpnec.2022.100139

Abstract

Modern human lifestyle strongly depends on complex social traits like empathy, tolerance, and cooperation. These diverse facets of social cognition have been associated with variation in the oxytocin receptor (*OTR*) and its sister genes, the vasotocin/vasopressin receptors (*VTR1A/AVPR1A* and *AVPR1B/VTR1B*). Here, we compared the available genomic sequences of these receptors between modern humans, archaic humans, and 12 non-human primate species, and identified sites that show heterozygous variation in modern humans and archaic humans distinct from variation in other primates, and for which we could find association studies with clinical implications. On these sites, we performed a range of analyses (variant clustering, pathogenicity prediction, regulation, linkage disequilibrium frequency) and reviewed the literature on selection data in different modern-human populations. We found five sites with modern human specific variation, where the modern human allele is the major allele in the global population (*OTR*: rs1042778, rs237885, rs6770632; *VTR1A*: rs10877969; *VTR1B*: rs33985287). Among them, variation in the *OTR*-rs6770632 site was predicted to be the most functional. Two alleles (*OTR*: rs59190448 and rs237888) present only in modern humans and archaic humans were putatively under positive selection in modern humans, with rs237888 predicted to be a highly functional site. Three sites showed convergent evolution between modern humans and bonobos (*OTR*: rs2228485 and rs237897; *VTR1A*: rs1042615), with *OTR*-rs2228485 ranking highly in terms of functionality and reported to be under balancing selection in modern humans (Schaschl, 2015). Our findings have implications for understanding hominid prosociality, as well as the similarities between modern human and bonobo social behavior.

High dream recall frequency is associated with increased creativity and default mode network connectivity

Vallat, R., Türker, B., Nicolas, A., & Ruby, P. (2022). High dream recall frequency is associated with increased creativity and default mode network connectivity. *Nature and Science of Sleep*, *14*, 265–275. doi:10.2147/NSS.S342137

Abstract

Introduction: Several results suggest that the frequency of dream recall is positively correlated with personality traits such as creativity and openness to experience. In addition, neuroimaging results have evidenced different neurophysiological profiles in high dream recallers (HR) and low dream recallers (LR) during both sleep and wakefulness, specifically within regions of the default mode network (DMN). These findings are consistent with the emerging view that dreaming and mind wandering pertain to the same family of spontaneous mental processes, subserved by the DMN.

Methods: To further test this hypothesis, we measured the DMN functional connectivity during resting wakefulness, together with personality and cognitive abilities (including creativity) in 28 HR and 27 LR.

Results: As expected, HR demonstrated a greater DMN connectivity than LR, higher scores of creativity, and no significant difference in memory abilities. However, there was no significant correlation between creativity scores and DMN connectivity.

Discussion: These results further demonstrate that there are trait neurophysiological and psychological differences between individuals who frequently recall their dreams and those who do not. They support the forebrain and the DMN hypotheses of dreaming and leave open the possibility that increased activity in the DMN promotes creative-thinking during both wakefulness and sleep. Further work is needed to test whether activity in the DMN is causally associated with creative-thinking.

Default-mode and task-positive network activity in major depressive disorder: Implications for adaptive and maladaptive rumination

Hamilton, J. P., Furman, D. J., Chang, C., Thomason, M. E., Dennis, E., & Gotlib, I. H. (2011). Default-mode and task-positive network activity in major depressive disorder: Implications for adaptive and maladaptive rumination. *Biological Psychiatry*, *70*(4), 327–333. doi:10.1016/j.biopsych.2011.02.003

Abstract

Background: Major depressive disorder (MDD) has been associated reliably with ruminative responding; this kind of responding is composed of both maladaptive and adaptive components. Levels of activity in the default-mode network (DMN) relative to the task-positive network (TPN), as well as activity in structures that influence DMN and TPN functioning, may represent important neural substrates of maladaptive and adaptive rumination in MDD.

Methods: We used a unique metric to estimate DMN dominance over TPN from blood oxygenation level-dependent data collected during eyes-closed rest in 17 currently depressed and 17 never-disordered adults. We calculated correlations between this metric of DMN dominance over TPN and the depressive, brooding, and reflective subscales of the Ruminative Responses Scale, correcting for associations between these measures both with one another and with severity of depression. Finally, we estimated and compared across groups right fronto-insular cortex (RFIC) response during initiations of ascent in DMN and in TPN activity.

Results: In the MDD participants, increasing levels of DMN dominance were associated with higher levels of maladaptive, depressive rumination and lower levels of adaptive, reflective rumination. Moreover, our RFIC state-change analysis showed increased RFIC activation in the MDD participants at the onset of increases in TPN activity; conversely, healthy control participants exhibited increased RFIC response at the onset of increases in DMN activity.

Conclusions: These findings support a formulation in which the DMN undergirds representation of negative, self-referential information in depression, and the RFIC, when prompted by increased levels of DMN activity, initiates an adaptive engagement of the TPN.

Anterior cingulate cortex in individuals with depressive symptoms: A structural MRI study

Ibrahim, H. M., Kulikova, A., Ly, H., Rush, A. J., & Brown, E. S. (2022). Anterior cingulate cortex in individuals with depressive symptoms: A structural MRI study. *Psychiatry Research: Neuroimaging, 319*, 111420. doi:10.1016/j.pscychresns.2021.111420

Abstract

Several magnetic resonance imaging (MRI) studies have reported reduction in anterior cingulate cortex (ACC) volume in individuals with major depressive disorder (MDD). However, some MRI studies did not find significant ACC volumetric changes in MDD, and sample sizes were generally small. This cross-sectional structural MRI study examined the relationship between current depressive symptoms and ACC volume in a large community sample of 1,803 adults. A series of multiple linear regression analyses were conducted to predict right and left ACC volumes using Quick Inventory of Depressive Symptomatology Self-Report (QIDS-SR) scores, intracranial volume, age, sex, race/ethnicity, alcohol use, tobacco use, and psychotropic medications as predictor variables. Right ACC volume was significantly negatively associated with QIDS-SR scores, while no significant association was found between left ACC volume and QIDS-SR scores. In addition, there was a significant negative association between QIDS-SR scores and right but not left ACC volumes in males, and no significant association between QIDS-SR scores and right or left ACC volumes in females. These findings suggest that right ACC volume is reduced in people with greater self-reported depressive symptom severity, and that this association is only significant in men.

Beneficial effects of motor imagery and self-talk on service performance in skilled tennis players

Robin, N., Dominique, L., Guillet-Descas, E., & Hue, O. (2022). Beneficial effects of motor imagery and self-talk on service performance in skilled tennis players. *Frontiers in Psychology*, 13, 778468. doi:10.3389/fpsyg.2022.778468

Abstract

This research aim to investigate the effects of motor imagery (MI), focused on the trajectory of the ball and the target area, and self-talk (motivational function) before the actual strike on the performance of the service in skilled tennis players. Thirty-three participants (6 females and 27 males, $M_{age} = 15.9$ years), competing in regional to national competitions, were randomly divided into three groups: Control, MI, and MI + self-talk. They performed a pretest (25 first service), 20 acquisition sessions (physical trial, physical trial + MI and physical trial + MI + self-talk), and a posttest similar to the pretest, in match situations. The percentage of the first service, their speed, and the efficiency scores, evaluated by experts, were use as dependent variables and indicators of performance. While there was no difference in service speed ($p > 0.05$), this study showed an improvement in the first service percentage and efficiency (all, $p < 0.01$) in the participants of the MI and MI + self-talk groups. Additionally, analyses revealed greater efficiency when MI was combined with self-talk compared to other conditions. It therefore seems advantageous for skilled tennis players to use MI and motivational self-talk before performing the first service balls.

Romantic attachment, stress, and cognitive functioning in a large sample of middle-aged and older couples

Weidmann, R., & Chopik, W. J. (2022). Romantic attachment, stress, and cognitive functioning in a large sample of middle-aged and older couples. *Journal of Research in Personality, 98*, 104233. doi:10.1016/j.jrp.2022.104233

Abstract

This study examined the link between insecure attachment and cognitive functioning in 1,043 middle-aged and older romantic couples ($M_{age} = 64.7$ years), and tests whether stress acts as a mediator. Participants were asked about their romantic attachment (anxiety and avoidance), cognitive impairment, their and their partner's dementia symptoms, and were tested on their memory performance. Findings suggest that anxiously attached individuals experience more stress and report worse cognitive functioning, while partners of avoidantly attached individuals experience more stress, report worse cognitive functioning, and show worse memory performance. Post-hoc robustness analyses suggest that relationship satisfaction accounts for the link between avoidance and stress and serves as a mediator. Insecure attachment reflects a potential risk for worse cognitive health in older couples.

Randomized manipulation of early cognitive experience impacts adult brain structure

Farah, M. J., Sternberg, S., Nichols, T. A., Duda, J. T., Lohrenz, T., Luo, Y., … Ramey, C. T. (2021). Randomized manipulation of early cognitive experience impacts adult brain structure. *Journal of Cognitive Neuroscience, 33*(6), 1197–1209. doi:10.1162/jocn_a_01709

Abstract

Does early exposure to cognitive and linguistic stimulation impact brain structure? Or do genetic predispositions account for the co-occurrence of certain neuroanatomical phenotypes and a tendency to engage children in cognitively stimulating activities? Low socioeconomic status infants were randomized to either five years of cognitively and linguistically stimulating center-based care or a comparison condition. The intervention resulted in large and statistically significant changes in brain structure measured in midlife, particularly for male individuals. These findings are the first to extend the large literature on cognitive enrichment effects on animal brains to humans, and to demonstrate the effects of uniquely human features such as linguistic stimulation.

The human brain in numbers: A linearly scaled-up primate brain

Herculano-Houzel, S. (2009). The human brain in numbers: A linearly scaled-up primate brain. *Frontiers in Human Neuroscience, 3,* 31. doi:10.3389/neuro.09.031.2009

Abstract

The human brain has often been viewed as outstanding among mammalian brains: the most cognitively able, the largest-than-expected from body size, endowed with an overdeveloped cerebral cortex that represents over 80% of brain mass, and purportedly containing 100 billion neurons and 10 times more glial cells. Such uniqueness was seemingly necessary to justify the superior cognitive abilities of humans over larger-brained mammals such as elephants and whales. However, our recent studies using a novel method to determine the cellular composition of the brain of humans and other primates as well as of rodents and insectivores show that, since different cellular scaling rules apply to the brains within these orders, brain size can no longer be considered a proxy for the number of neurons in the brain. These studies also showed that the human brain is not exceptional in its cellular composition, as it was found to contain as many neuronal and non-neuronal cells as would be expected of a primate brain of its size. Additionally, the so-called overdeveloped human cerebral cortex holds only 19% of all brain neurons, a fraction that is similar to that found in other mammals. Regarding absolute numbers of neurons, however, the human brain does have two advantages compared to other mammalian brains: compared to rodents, and probably to whales and elephants as well, it is built according to the very economical, space-saving scaling rules that apply to other primates; and, among economically built primate brains, it is the largest, hence containing the most neurons. These findings argue in favor of a view of cognitive abilities that is centered on absolute numbers of neurons, rather than on body size or encephalization, and call for a reexamination of several concepts related to the exceptionality of the human brain.

This is your brain in meltdown

Arnsten, A., Mazure, C. M., & Sinha, R. (2012). This is your brain in meltdown. *Scientific American, 306*(4), 48–53. doi:10.1038/scientificamerican0412-48

Abstract

The entrance exam to medical school consists of a five-hour fusillade of hundreds of questions that, even with the best preparation, often leaves the test taker discombobulated and anxious. For some would-be physicians, the relentless pressure causes their reasoning abilities to slow and even shut down entirely. The experience—known variously as choking, brain freeze, nerves, jitters, folding, blanking out, the yips or a dozen other descriptive terms—is all too familiar to virtually anyone who has flubbed a speech, bumped up against writer's block or struggled through a lengthy exam.

Beyond dimension reduction: Stable electric fields emerge from and allow representational drift

Pinotsis, D. A., & Miller, E. K. (2022). Beyond dimension reduction: Stable electric fields emerge from and allow representational drift. *NeuroImage, 253*, 119058. doi:10.1016/j.neuroimage.2022.119058

Abstract
It is known that the exact neurons maintaining a given memory (the neural ensemble) change from trial to trial. This raises the question of how the brain achieves stability in the face of this representational drift. Here, we demonstrate that this stability emerges at the level of the electric fields that arise from neural activity. We show that electric fields carry information about working memory content. The electric fields, in turn, can act as "guard rails" that funnel higher dimensional variable neural activity along stable lower dimensional routes. We obtained the latent space associated with each memory. We then confirmed the stability of the electric field by mapping the latent space to different cortical patches (that comprise a neural ensemble) and reconstructing information flow between patches. Stable electric fields can allow latent states to be transferred between brain areas, in accord with modern engram theory.

Olfactory bulb volume and cortical thickness evolve during sommelier training

Filiz, G., Poupon, D., Banks, S., Fernandez, P., & Frasnelli, J. (2022). Olfactory bulb volume and cortical thickness evolve during sommelier training. *Human Brain Mapping, 43*(8), 2621–2633. doi:10.1002/hbm.25809

Abstract
Brain plasticity is essential for experts to acquire the abilities they need. Sommeliers are olfaction experts who display differences in olfactory regions in the brain that correlate with greater olfactory abilities. While most studies on this topic are cross-sectional, we used a longitudinal design and invited 17 sommelier students at the start and end of their training then to compare them to 17 control students to study the effects of training-related brain plasticity. After a year and a half, 5 sommelier students and 4 control students dropped out, leading to 12 sommelier students versus 13 controls. We used magnetic resonance imaging to measure cortical thickness and olfactory bulb volume, as this structure plays a crucial role in olfactory processing. We used the Sniffin' Sticks test to evaluate olfactory performance. During training, olfactory bulb volume increased in sommelier students while there was no significant change in the control group. We also observed that thickness of right entorhinal cortex increased, and cortical thickness decreased in other cerebral regions. Our olfactory tests did not reveal any significant changes in sommelier students. In conclusion, this is the first longitudinal study to report an increase in olfactory bulb volume in olfaction experts in line with the notion of effects of ecological training-related brain plasticity. The mixed results about cortical thickness might be explained by an "overproduction-pruning" model of brain plasticity, according to which the effects of training-related plasticity are non-linear and simultaneously involve different processes.

Shared cognitive mechanisms of hypnotizability with executive functioning and information salience

Faerman, A., & Spiegel, D. (2021). Shared cognitive mechanisms of hypnotizability with executive functioning and information salience. *Scientific Reports, 11*(1), 5704. doi:10.1038/s41598-021-84954-8

Abstract
In recent years, evidence linked hypnotizability to the executive control and information salience networks, brain structures that play a role in cognitive conflict resolution and perseveration (insisting on applying a previously learned logical rule on a new set). Despite the growing body of neuroimaging evidence, the cognitive phenotype

of hypnotizability is not well understood. We hypothesized that higher hypnotizability would correspond to lower perseveration and set-shifting. Seventy-two healthy adults were tested for hypnotizability and executive functions (perseveration and set-shifting). Multiple regression analyses were performed to test the relationship between hypnotizability and perseveration and set-shifting. Higher hypnotizability was associated with lower perseveration after accounting for age and education. Hypnotizability significantly predicted perseveration but not set-shifting. Our results indicate an inverse relationship between trait hypnotizability and perseveration, an executive function that utilizes regions of both the executive control and the salience systems. This suggests that hypnotizability may share a common cognitive mechanism with error evaluation and implementation of logical rules.

Stimulation of the ventromedial prefrontal cortex blocks the return of subcortically mediated fear responses

Szeska, C., Pünjer, H., Riemann, S., Meinzer, M., & Hamm, A. O. (2022). Stimulation of the ventromedial prefrontal cortex blocks the return of subcortically mediated fear responses. *Translational Psychiatry*, *12*(1), 394. doi:10.1038/s41398-022-02174-8

Abstract

The ventromedial prefrontal cortex (vmPFC) mediates the inhibition of defensive responses upon encounters of cues that had lost their attribute as a threat signal via previous extinction learning. Here, we investigated whether such fear extinction recall can be facilitated by anodal transcranial direct current stimulation (tDCS). Extinction recall was tested 24 hours after previously acquired fear was extinguished. Either anodal tDCS or sham stimulation targeting the vmPFC was applied during this test. After stimulation ceased, we examined return of fear after subjects had been re-exposed to aversive events. Fear was assessed by reports of threat expectancy and modulations of autonomic (skin conductance, heart rate) and protective reflex (startle potentiation) measures, the latter of which are mediated by subcortical defense circuits. While tDCS did not affect initial extinction recall, it abolished the return of startle potentiation and autonomic components of the fear response. Results suggest hierarchical multi-level vmPFC functions in human fear inhibition and indicate that its stimulation might immunize against relapses into pathological subcortically mediated defensive activation.

CANCER

The efficacy of photobiomodulation therapy in improving tissue resilience and healing of radiation skin damage

Mosca, R. C., Santos, S. N., Nogueira, G. E. C., Pereira, D. L., Costa, F. C., Pereira, J. X., … Arany, P. R. (2021). The efficacy of photobiomodulation therapy in improving tissue resilience and healing of radiation skin damage. *Photonics, 9*(1), 10. doi:10.3390/photonics9010010

Abstract

The increased precision, efficacy, and safety of radiation brachytherapy has tremendously improved its popularity in cancer care. However, an unfortunate side effect of this therapy involves localized skin damage and breakdown that are managed palliatively currently. This study was motivated by prior reports on the efficacy of photobiomodulation (PBM) therapy in improving tissue resilience and wound healing. We evaluated the efficacy of PBM therapy on 36 athymic mice with ^{125}I seed (0.42 mCi) implantation over 60 days. PBM treatments were performed with either red (660 nm) or near-infrared (880 nm, NIR) LEDs irradiance of 40 mW/cm^2, continuous wave, fluence of 20 J/cm^2 once per week. Animals were evaluated every 7 days with digital imaging, laser Doppler flowmetry, thermal imaging, μPET-CT imaging using ^{18}F-FDG, and histology. We observed that both PBM treatments—red and NIR—demonstrated significantly less incidence and severity and improved healing with skin radionecrosis. Radiation exposed tissues had improved functional parameters such as vascular perfusion, reduced inflammation, and metabolic derangement following PBM therapy. Histological analysis confirmed these observations with minimal damage and resolution in tissues exposed to radiation. To our knowledge, this is the first report on the successful use of PBM therapy for brachytherapy. The results from this study support future mechanistic lab studies and controlled human clinical studies to utilize this innovative therapy in managing side effects from radiation cancer treatments.

Rapid and sustained symptom reduction following psilocybin treatment for anxiety and depression in patients with life-threatening cancer: A randomized controlled trial

Ross, S., Bossis, A., Guss, J., Agin-Liebes, G., Malone, T., Cohen, B., ... Schmidt, B. L. (2016). Rapid and sustained symptom reduction following psilocybin treatment for anxiety and depression in patients with life-threatening cancer: A randomized controlled trial. *Journal of Psychopharmacology, 30*(12), 1165–1180. doi:10.1177/0269881116675512

Abstract

Background: Clinically significant anxiety and depression are common in patients with cancer, and are associated with poor psychiatric and medical outcomes. Historical and recent research suggests a role for psilocybin to treat cancer-related anxiety and depression.

Methods: In this double-blind, placebo-controlled, crossover trial, 29 patients with cancer-related anxiety and depression were randomly assigned and received treatment with single-dose psilocybin (0.3 mg/kg) or niacin, both in conjunction with psychotherapy. The primary outcomes were anxiety and depression assessed between groups prior to the crossover at 7 weeks.

Results: Prior to the crossover, psilocybin produced immediate, substantial, and sustained improvements in anxiety and depression and led to decreases in cancer-related demoralization and hopelessness, improved spiritual well-being, and increased quality of life. At the 6.5-month follow-up, psilocybin was associated with enduring anxiolytic and antidepressant effects (approximately 60–80% of participants continued with clinically significant reductions in depression or anxiety), sustained benefits in existential distress and quality of life, as well as improved attitudes towards death. The psilocybin-induced mystical experience mediated the therapeutic effect of psilocybin on anxiety and depression.

Conclusions: In conjunction with psychotherapy, single moderate-dose psilocybin produced rapid, robust and enduring anxiolytic and antidepressant effects in patients with cancer-related psychological distress.

ENVIRONMENT

Exposure to unconventional oil and gas development and all-cause mortality in Medicare beneficiaries

Li, L., Dominici, F., Blomberg, A. J., Bargagli-Stoffi, F. J., Schwartz, J. D., Coull, B. A., ... Koutrakis, P. (2022). Exposure to unconventional oil and gas development and all-cause mortality in Medicare beneficiaries. *Nature Energy*, *7*(2), 177–185. doi:10.1038/s41560-021-00970-y

Abstract

Little is known about whether exposure to unconventional oil and gas development is associated with higher mortality risks in the elderly and whether related air pollutants are exposure pathways. We studied a cohort of 15,198,496 Medicare beneficiaries (136,215,059 person-years) in all major US unconventional exploration regions from 2001 to 2015. We gathered data from records of more than 2.5 million oil and gas wells. For each beneficiary's zip code of residence and year in the cohort, we calculated a proximity-based and a downwind-based pollutant exposure. We analyzed the data using two methods: Cox proportional hazards model and Difference-in-Differences. We found evidence of statistically significant higher mortality risk associated with living in proximity to and downwind of unconventional oil and gas wells. Our results suggest that primary air pollutants sourced from unconventional oil and gas exploration can be a major exposure pathway with adverse health effects in the elderly.

How nature nurtures: Amygdala activity decreases as the result of a one-hour walk in nature

Sudimac, S., Sale, V., & Kühn, S. (2022). How nature nurtures: Amygdala activity decreases as the result of a one-hour walk in nature. *Molecular Psychiatry, 27*(11), 4446–4452. doi:10.1038/s41380-022-01720-6

Abstract

Since living in cities is associated with an increased risk for mental disorders such as anxiety disorders, depression, and schizophrenia, it is essential to understand how exposure to urban and natural environments affects mental health and the brain. It has been shown that the amygdala is more activated during a stress task in urban compared to rural dwellers. However, no study so far has examined the causal effects of natural and urban environments on stress-related brain mechanisms. To address this question, we conducted an intervention study to investigate changes in stress-related brain regions as an effect of a one-hour walk in an urban (busy street) vs. natural environment (forest). Brain activation was measured in 63 healthy participants, before and after the walk, using a fearful faces task and a social stress task. Our findings reveal that amygdala activation decreases after the walk in nature, whereas it remains stable after the walk in an urban environment. These results suggest that going for a walk in nature can have salutogenic effects on stress-related brain regions, and consequently, it may act as a preventive measure against mental strain and potentially disease. Given rapidly increasing urbanization, the present results may influence urban planning to create more accessible green areas and to adapt urban environments in a way that will be beneficial for citizens' mental health.

Smartphone-based ecological momentary assessment reveals mental health benefits of birdlife

Hammoud, R., Tognin, S., Burgess, L., Bergou, N., Smythe, M., Gibbons, J., … Mechelli, A. (2022). Smartphone-based ecological momentary assessment reveals mental health benefits of birdlife. *Scientific Reports*, *12*(1), 17589. doi:10.1038/s41598-022-20207-6

Abstract

The mental health benefits of everyday encounters with birdlife for mental health are poorly understood. Previous studies have typically relied on retrospective questionnaires or artificial set-ups with little ecological validity. In the present study, we used the Urban Mind smartphone application to examine the impact of seeing or hearing birds on self-reported mental wellbeing in real-life contexts. A sample of 1,292 participants completed a total of 26,856 ecological momentary assessments between April 2018 and October 2021. Everyday encounters with birdlife were associated with time-lasting improvements in mental wellbeing. These improvements were evident not only in healthy people but also in those with a diagnosis of depression, the most common mental illness across the world. These findings have potential implications for both environmental and wildlife protection and mental healthcare policies. Specific measures, aimed at preserving and increasing everyday encounters with birdlife in urban areas, should be implemented.

MECHANISMS

Personality traits relate to chronotype at both the phenotypic and genetic level

Lenneis, A., Vainik, U., Teder-Laving, M., Ausmees, L., Lemola, S., Allik, J., & Realo, A. (2021). Personality traits relate to chronotype at both the phenotypic and genetic level. *Journal of Personality*, *89*(6), 1206–1222. doi:10.1111/jopy.12645

Abstract

Introduction: Diurnal preferences have been linked to personality but often with mixed results. The present study examines the relationships between sleep timing (chronotype), diurnal preferences, and the Five-Factor Model of personality traits at the phenotypic and genetic level.

Methods: Self- and informant-reports of the NEO Personality Inventory-3, self-reports of the Munich Chronotype Questionnaire, and DNA samples were available for 2,515 Estonian adults (M_{age} = 45.76 years; 59% females). Genetic correlations were obtained through summary statistics of genome-wide association studies.

Results: Results showed that higher Conscientiousness and lower Openness to Experience were significant predictors of earlier chronotype. At the level of facets, we found that more straightforward (A2) and excitement-seeking (E5), yet less self-disciplined (C5) people were more likely to have later chronotypes. The nuance-level Polypersonality score was correlated with chronotype at $r = .28$ ($p < .001$). Conscientiousness and Openness were genetically related with diurnal preferences. The polygenic score for morningness-eveningness significantly predicted the Polypersonality score.

Conclusion: Phenotypic measures of chronotype and personality showed significant associations at all three of levels of the personality hierarchy. Our findings indicate that the relationship between personality and morningness-eveningness is partly due to genetic factors. Future studies are necessary to further refine the relationship.

Longitudinal associations between attachment, differentiation of self, and couple sexual and relational outcomes

Allsop, D. B., Price, A. A., Hanna-Walker, V., Leavitt, C. E., Milius, E. H., & Driggs, S. M. (2021). Longitudinal associations between attachment, differentiation of self, and couple sexual and relational outcomes. *Sexual and Relationship Therapy*, 1–20. doi:10.1080/14681994.2021.2003320

Abstract

We explored longitudinal associations between attachment, differentiation, relational satisfaction, and sexual satisfaction and desire among 286 married couples to see which of the two differing domains of attachment and differentiation of self best predict couple relationship outcomes. We observed that baseline attachment variables did not significantly predict couple sexual outcomes a year later while differentiation variables did. Specifically, husbands' emotional cutoff predicted decreased husbands' sexual desire and wives' emotional reactivity predicted decreased wives' sexual desire. Additionally, wives' emotional cutoff predicted increased wives' avoidant attachment and husbands' avoidant attachment predicted decreased wives' emotional cutoff. Implications for practitioners are discussed.

Is it painful? Playing violent video games affects brain responses to painful pictures: An event-related potential study

Miedzobrodzka, E., van Hooff, J. C., Konijn, E. A., & Krabbendam, L. (2022). Is it painful? Playing violent video games affects brain responses to painful pictures: An event-related potential study. *Psychology of Popular Media*, *11*(1), 13–23. doi:10.1037/ppm0000290

Abstract

Previous research showed mixed evidence on how violent video game exposure (VVGE) may affect empathy for pain in the brain. This study applied an event-related potential (ERP) approach to improve understanding of how habitual and short-term violent game play may affect top-down and bottom-up empathy for pain brain responses. A total of 58 male participants with different levels of habitual VVGE performed a pain judgment task before and after 40 minutes of violent game play while their brain responses were recorded. Results showed that only late cognitive-evaluative ERP responses (P3, P625) were sensitive to the pictures' painfulness, which were also affected by both habitual VVGE and short-term violent game play. As expected, participants with no habitual VVGE showed an ERP pain effect before game play: higher P3 and P625 amplitudes for painful versus nonpainful pictures. In contrast, a similar ERP pain effect was not observed in participants with high VVGE before game play, suggesting habitual desensitization. Short-term violent game play resulted in lower P3 and P625 amplitudes for painful pictures in the no VVGE group, indicating short-term desensitization. We discuss the observed VVGE desensitization effects in terms of top-down regulation of an empathetic response induced by painful stimuli. Though such adaptation could be beneficial in a violent game environment, possible long-term consequences associated with reduced empathic responsiveness in a social context should be further studied. In all, our findings contribute to the debate on the effects of VVGE on the brain by providing first ERP evidence suggesting empathy for pain desensitization.

Motivating personal growth by seeking discomfort

Woolley, K., & Fishbach, A. (2022). Motivating personal growth by seeking discomfort. *Psychological Science, 33*(4), 510–523. doi:10.1177/09567976211044685

Abstract

Achieving personal growth often requires experiencing discomfort. What if instead of tolerating discomfort (e.g., feeling awkward or uncomfortable), people actively sought it out? Because discomfort is usually experienced immediately and is easy to detect, we suggest that seeking discomfort as a signal of growth can increase motivation. Five experiments (total $N = 2{,}163$ adults) tested this prediction across various areas of personal growth: taking improvisation classes to increase self-confidence, engaging in expressive writing to process difficult emotions, becoming informed about the COVID-19 health crisis, opening oneself to opposing political viewpoints, and learning about gun violence. Across these areas of personal development, seeking discomfort as a signal of self-growth motivated engagement and increased perceived goal achievement relative to standard instructions. Consistent with our theorizing, results showed that these effects occurred only in areas of personal growth that cause immediate discomfort.

Body shape matters: Evidence from machine learning on body shape-income relationship

Song, S., & Baek, S. (2021). Body shape matters: Evidence from machine learning on body shape-income relationship. *PLoS One, 16*(7), e0254785. doi:10.1371/journal.pone.0254785

Abstract

The association between physical appearance and income has been of central interest in social science. However, most previous studies often measured physical appearance using classical proxies from subjective opinions based on surveys. In this study, we use novel data, called CAESAR, which contains three-dimensional (3D) whole-body scans to mitigate possible reporting and measurement errors. We demonstrate the existence of significant nonclassical reporting errors in the reported heights and weights by comparing them with measured counterparts, and show that these discrete measurements are too sparse to provide a complete description of the body shape. Instead, we use a graphical autoencoder to obtain intrinsic features, consisting of human body shapes directly from 3D scans and estimate the relationship between body shapes and family income. We also take into account a possible issue of endogenous body shapes using proxy variables and control functions. The estimation results reveal a statistically significant relationship between physical appearance and family income and that these associations differ across genders. This supports the hypothesis on the physical attractiveness premium in labor market outcomes and its heterogeneity across genders.

PAIN

Exploring lumbar and lower limb kinematics and kinetics for evidence that lifting technique is associated with LBP

Saraceni, N., Campbell, A., Kent, P., Ng, L., Straker, L., & O'Sullivan, P. (2021). Exploring lumbar and lower limb kinematics and kinetics for evidence that lifting technique is associated with LBP. *PLoS One, 16*(7), e0254241. doi:10.1371/journal.pone.0254241

Abstract

Purpose: To investigate if lumbar and lower limb kinematics or kinetics are different between groups with and without a history of lower back pain (LBP) during lifting. Secondly, to investigate relationships between biomechanical variables and pain ramp during repeated lifting.

Methods: 21 LBP and 20 noLBP participants completed a 100-lift task, where lumbar and lower limb kinematics and kinetics were measured during lifting, with a simultaneous report of LBP intensity every 10 lifts. Lifts were performed in a laboratory setting, limiting ecological validity.

Results: The LBP group used a different lifting technique to the noLBP group at the beginning of the task (slower and more squat-like). Kinetic differences at the beginning included less peak lumbar external anterior shear force and greater peak knee power demonstrated by the LBP group. However, at the end of the task, both groups lifted with a much more similar technique that could be classified as more stoop-like and faster. Peak knee power remained greater in the LBP group throughout and was the only kinetic difference between groups at the end of the lifting task. While both groups lifted using a more comparable technique at the end, the LBP group still demonstrated a tendency to perform a slower and more squat-like lift throughout the task. Only one of 21 variables (pelvic tilt at box lift-off) was associated with pain ramp in the LBP group.

Conclusions: Workers with a history of LBP, lift with a style that is slower and more squat-like than workers without any history of LBP. Common assumptions that LBP is associated with lumbar kinematics or kinetics such as greater lumbar flexion or greater forces were not observed in this study, raising questions about the current paradigm around "safe lifting."

PTSD/TRAUMA

Relationship between early-life stress and trait mindfulness in adulthood: A correlational study

de Moraes, V. S., Fernandes, M., Fernandes, M. N. D. F., Gimenez, L. B. H., Camargo Júnior, E. B., & Gherardi-Donato, E. C. D. S. (2020). Relationship between early-life stress and trait mindfulness in adulthood: A correlational study. *BMC Psychology*, *11*(1), 15. doi:10.1186/s40359-022-01029-7

Abstract
Background: To investigate the relationship between early-life stress (ELS) and the trait mindfulness level in workers.

Method: This study is quantitative cross-sectional and correlational research with a sample of 929 workers from a Brazilian public university. ELS and mindfulness assessment was performed using the Childhood Trauma Questionnaire (CTQ) and the Five-Facet Mindfulness Questionnaire-BR (FFMQ-BR), respectively. The data were submitted to correlation tests adopting a significance level of .05 and a multivariate linear regression analysis.

Results: 50.0% of the participants obtained a score indicative of ELS exposure in at least one subtype among the five proposed by the CTQ, with emotional neglect predominating (63.0%). The group not exposed to emotional abuse had higher scores in the "describe-positive formulation" and "non-reactivity to inner experience" facets. Those that scored for physical abuse had higher values in "acting with awareness-autopilot." However, the group exposed to sexual abuse obtained the highest score in the "acting with awareness-autopilot" and "acting with awareness-distraction" facets. The correlation between FFMQ-BR and CTQ overall scores showed a weak correlation with statistical significance. The multiple linear revealed that the facets of mindfulness were significantly associated by at least one type of early stress; however, no significant association was found between CTQ and FFMQ-BR overall results.

Conclusion: The results showed that emotional regulation might have effectively occurred in this specific population, even with the presence of some childhood trauma.

The impact of ACEs on BMI: An investigation of the genotype-environment effects of BMI

Schlauch, K. A., Read, R. W., Neveux, I., Lipp, B., Slonim, A., & Grzymski, J. J. (2022). The impact of ACEs on BMI: An investigation of the genotype-environment effects of BMI. *Frontiers in Genetics*, *13*, 816660. doi:10.3389/fgene.2022.816660

Abstract

Adverse Childhood Experiences (ACEs) are stressful and traumatic events occurring before the age of eighteen shown to cause mental and physical health problems, including increased risk of obesity. Obesity remains an ongoing national challenge with no predicted solution. We examine a subset of the Healthy Nevada Project, focusing on a multi-ethnic cohort of 15,886 sequenced participants with recalled adverse childhood events, to study how ACEs and their genotype-environment interactions affect BMI. Specifically, the Healthy Nevada Project participants sequenced by the Helix Exome+ platform were cross-referenced to their electronic medical records and social health determinants questionnaire to identify: 1) the effect of ACEs on BMI in the absence of genetics; 2) the effect of genotype-environment interactions on BMI; 3) how these gene-environment interactions differ from standard genetic associations of BMI. The study found very strong significant associations between the number of adverse childhood experiences and adult obesity. Additionally, we identified 55 common and rare variants that exhibited gene-interaction effects including three variants in the *CAMK1D* gene and four variants in *LHPP*; both genes are linked to schizophrenia. Surprisingly, none of the variants identified with interactive effects were in canonical obesity-related genes. Here we show the delicate balance between genes and environment, and how the two strongly influence each other.

Treatment patterns of anxiety and posttraumatic stress disorder following traumatic brain injury

Marks, M. R., Dux, M. C., Rao, V., & Albrecht, J. S. (2022). Treatment patterns of anxiety and posttraumatic stress disorder following traumatic brain injury. *Journal of Neuropsychiatry and Clinical Neurosciences*, *34*(3), 247–253. doi:10.1176/appi.neuropsych.21040104

Abstract

Objective: Symptoms of mental disorders are common, are underrecognized, and contribute to worse outcomes after traumatic brain injury (TBI). Post-TBI, prevalence of anxiety disorders and prevalence of posttraumatic stress disorder (PTSD) are comparable with that of depression, but evidence-based treatment guidelines are lacking. The investigators examined psychotropic medication use and psychotherapy patterns among individuals diagnosed with anxiety disorders and PTSD post-TBI.

Methods: Administrative claims data were used to compare the prevalence and patterns of pharmacotherapy and psychotherapy utilization among individuals diagnosed with an anxiety disorder or PTSD post-TBI.

Results: Among 207,354 adults with TBI, prevalence of anxiety disorders was 20.5%, and prevalence of PTSD was 0.6% post-TBI. Receipt of pharmacotherapy pre- and post-TBI (anxiety: pre-TBI = 58.4%, post-TBI = 76.2%; PTSD: pre-TBI = 53.7%, post-TBI = 75.2%) was considerably more common than receipt of psychotherapy (anxiety: pre-TBI = 5.8%, post-TBI = 19.1%; PTSD: pre-TBI = 11.2%, post-TBI = 36.0%). Individuals diagnosed with anxiety were 66% less likely to receive psychotherapy compared with individuals diagnosed with PTSD, although engagement in psychotherapy decreased faster over time among those with PTSD. Overall, psychotropic medication use and rates of antidepressant prescription use in the anxiety group were higher compared with those in the PTSD group. Benzodiazepines were the second most commonly prescribed medication class in the anxiety group, even though judicious use is warranted post-TBI.

Conclusions: Further exploration of differences and risks associated with pharmacotherapy for anxiety and PTSD post-TBI is warranted to refine treatment guidelines. The low level of psychotherapy engagement suggests that barriers and facilitators to psychotherapy utilization post-TBI should be examined in future studies.

OTHER HEALTH ISSUES

Psychiatric comorbidity and risk of premature mortality and suicide among those with chronic respiratory diseases, cardiovascular diseases, and diabetes in Sweden: A nationwide matched cohort study of over 1 million patients and their unaffected siblings

Sariaslan, A., Sharpe, M., Larsson, H., Wolf, A., Lichtenstein, P., & Fazel, S. (2022). Psychiatric comorbidity and risk of premature mortality and suicide among those with chronic respiratory diseases, cardiovascular diseases, and diabetes in Sweden: A nationwide matched cohort study of over 1 million patients and their unaffected siblings. *PLoS Medicine*, *19*(1), e1003864. doi:10.1371/journal.pmed.1003864

Abstract

Background: Persons with noncommunicable diseases have elevated rates of premature mortality. The contribution of psychiatric comorbidity to this is uncertain. We aimed to determine the risks of premature mortality and suicide in people with common noncommunicable diseases, with and without psychiatric disorder comorbidity.

Methods and findings: We used nationwide registries to study all individuals born in Sweden between 1932 and 1995 with inpatient and outpatient diagnoses of chronic respiratory diseases (n = 249,825), cardiovascular diseases (n = 568,818), and diabetes (n = 255,579) for risks of premature mortality (≤ age 65 years) and suicide until 31 December 2013. Patients diagnosed with either chronic respiratory diseases, cardiovascular diseases, or diabetes were compared with age and sex-matched population controls (n = 10,345,758) and unaffected biological full siblings (n = 1,119,543). Comorbidity with any psychiatric disorder, and by major psychiatric categories, was examined using diagnoses from patient registers. Associations were quantified using stratified Cox regression models that accounted for time at risk, measured sociodemographic factors, and unmeasured familial confounders via sibling comparisons. Within 5 years of diagnosis, at least 7% (range 7.4% to 10.8%; $p < 0.001$) of patients with respiratory diseases, cardiovascular diseases, or diabetes (median age at diagnosis: 48 to 54 years) had died from any cause, and 0.3% (0.3% to 0.3%; $p < 0.001$) had died from suicide, 25% to 32% of people with these medical conditions had co-occurring lifetime diagnoses of any psychiatric disorder, most of which antedated the medical diagnosis. Comorbid psychiatric disorders were associated with higher all-cause mortality (15.4% to 21.1%) when compared to those without such conditions (5.5% to 9.1%). Suicide mortality was also elevated (1.2% to 1.6% in comorbid patients versus 0.1% to 0.1% without comorbidity). When we compared relative risks with siblings without noncommunicable diseases and psychiatric disorders, the comorbidity with any psychiatric disorder was associated with substantially increased mortality rates (adjusted HR range: aHRCR = 7.2 [95% CI: 6.8 to 7.7; $p < 0.001$] to aHRCV = 8.9 [95% CI: 8.5 to 9.4; $p < 0.001$]). Notably, comorbid substance use disorders were associated with a higher mortality rate (aHR range: aHRCR = 8.3 [95% CI: 7.6 to 9.1; $p < 0.001$] to aHRCV = 9.9 [95% CI: 9.3 to 10.6; $p < 0.001$]) than depression (aHR range: aHRCR = 5.3 [95% CI: 4.7 to 5.9; $p < 0.001$] to aHRCV = 7.4 [95% CI: 7.0 to 7.9; $p < 0.001$]), but risks of suicide were similar for these two psychiatric comorbidities. One limitation is that we relied on secondary care data to assess psychiatric comorbidities, which may have led to missing some patients with less severe comorbidities. Residual genetic confounding is another limitation, given that biological full siblings share an average of half of their cosegregating genes. However, the reported associations remained large even after adjustment for shared and unmeasured familial confounders.

Conclusions: In this longitudinal study of over 1 million patients with chronic health diseases, we observed increased risks of all-cause and suicide mortality in individuals with psychiatric comorbidities. Improving assessment, treatment, and follow-up of people with comorbid psychiatric disorders may reduce the risk of mortality in people with chronic noncommunicable diseases.

Interplay of dinner timing and MTNR1B type 2 diabetes risk variant on glucose tolerance and insulin secretion: A randomized crossover trial.

Garaulet, M., Lopez-Minguez, J., Dashti, H. S., Vetter, C., Hernández-Martínez, A. M., Pérez-Ayala, M., … Saxena, R. (2022). Interplay of dinner timing and MTNR1B type 2 diabetes risk variant on glucose tolerance and insulin secretion: A randomized crossover trial. *Diabetes Care, 45*(3), 512–519. doi:10.2337/dc21-1314

Abstract

Objective: We tested whether the concurrence of food intake and elevated concentrations of endogenous melatonin, as occurs with late eating, results in impaired glucose control, in particular in carriers of the type 2 diabetes-associated G allele in the melatonin receptor-1B gene (MTNR1B).

Research design and methods: In a Spanish natural late-eating population, a randomized, crossover study was performed. Each participant ($n = 845$) underwent two evening 2-h 75-g oral glucose tolerance tests following an 8-hour fast: an early condition scheduled 4 hours prior to habitual bedtime ("early dinner timing") and a late condition scheduled 1 hour prior to habitual bedtime ("late dinner timing"), simulating an early and a late dinner timing, respectively. Differences in postprandial glucose and insulin responses between early and late dinner timing were determined using incremental area under the curve (AUC) calculated by the trapezoidal method.

Results: Melatonin serum levels were 3.5-fold higher in the late versus early condition, with late dinner timing resulting in 6.7% lower insulin AUC and 8.3% higher glucose AUC. The effect of late eating impairing glucose tolerance was stronger in the MTNR1B G-allele carriers than in noncarriers. Genotype differences in glucose tolerance were attributed to reductions in β-cell function (P for interaction, Pint glucose area under the curve = 0.009, Pint corrected insulin response = 0.022, and Pint disposition index = 0.018).

Conclusions: Concurrently high endogenous melatonin and carbohydrate intake, as typical for late eating, impairs glucose tolerance, especially in MTNR1B G-risk allele carriers, attributable to insulin secretion defects.

A metabolomics comparison of plant-based meat and grass-fed meat indicates large nutritional differences despite comparable Nutrition Facts panels

van Vliet, S., Bain, J. R., Muehlbauer, M. J., Provenza, F. D., Kronberg, S. L., Pieper, C. F., & Huffman, K. M. (2021). A metabolomics comparison of plant-based meat and grass-fed meat indicates large nutritional differences despite comparable Nutrition Facts panels. *Scientific Reports, 11*(1), 1–13. doi:10.1038/s41598-021-93100-3

Abstract

A new generation of plant-based meat alternatives-formulated to mimic the taste and nutritional composition of red meat-have attracted considerable consumer interest, research attention, and media coverage. This has raised questions of whether plant-based meat alternatives represent proper nutritional replacements to animal meat. The goal of our study was to use untargeted metabolomics to provide an in-depth comparison of the metabolite profiles a popular plant-based meat alternative ($n = 18$) and grass-fed ground beef ($n = 18$) matched for serving size (113 g) and fat content (14 g). Despite apparent similarities based on Nutrition Facts panels, our metabolomics analysis found that metabolite abundances between the plant-based meat alternative and grass-fed ground beef differed by 90% (171 out of 190 profiled metabolites; false discovery rate adjusted $p < 0.05$). Several metabolites were found either exclusively (22 metabolites) or in greater quantities in beef (51 metabolites) (all, $p < 0.05$). Nutrients such as docosahexaenoic acid (ω-3), niacinamide (vitamin B3), glucosamine, hydroxyproline and the anti-oxidants allantoin, anserine, cysteamine, spermine, and squalene were amongst those only found in beef. Several other metabolites were found exclusively (31 metabolites) or in greater quantities (67 metabolites) in the plant-based meat alternative (all, $p < 0.05$). Ascorbate (vitamin C), phytosterols, and several phenolic anti-oxidants such as loganin, sulfurol, syringic acid, tyrosol, and vanillic acid were amongst those only found in the plant-based meat alternative. Large differences in metabolites within various nutrient classes (e.g., amino acids, dipeptides, vitamins, phenols, tocopherols, and fatty acids) with physiological, anti-inflammatory, and/or immunomodulatory roles indicate that these products should not be viewed as truly nutritionally interchangeable, but could be viewed as complementary in terms of provided nutrients. The new information we provide is important for making informed decisions by consumers and health professionals. It cannot be determined from our data if either source is healthier to consume.

Impact of weight loss on brain age: Improved brain health following bariatric surgery

Zeighami, Y., Dadar, M., Daoust, J., Pelletier, M., Biertho, L., Bouvet-Bouchard, L., … Michaud, A. (2022). Impact of weight loss on brain age: Improved brain health following bariatric surgery. *NeuroImage*, *259*, 119415. doi:10.1016/j.neuroimage.2022.119415

Abstract

Individuals living with obesity tend to have increased brain age, reflecting poorer brain health likely due to grey and white matter atrophy related to obesity. However, it is unclear if older brain age associated with obesity can be reversed following weight loss and cardiometabolic health improvement. The aim of this study was to assess the impact of weight loss and cardiometabolic improvement following bariatric surgery on brain health, as measured by change in brain age estimated based on voxel-based morphometry (VBM) measurements. We used three distinct datasets to perform this study: 1) CamCAN dataset to train the brain age prediction model; 2) Human Connectome Project (HCP) dataset to investigate whether individuals with obesity have greater brain age than individuals with normal weight; and 3) pre-surgery, as well as 4, 12, and 24 month post-surgery data from participants (n = 87, age: 44.0 ± 9.2 years, BMI: 43.9 ± 4.2 kg/m^2) who underwent a bariatric surgery to investigate whether weight loss and cardiometabolic improvement as a result of bariatric surgery lowers the brain age. As expected, our results from the HCP dataset showed a higher brain age for individuals with obesity compared to individuals with normal weight (T-value = 7.08, $p < 0.0001$). We also found significant improvement in brain health, indicated by a decrease of 2.9 and 5.6 years in adjusted delta age at 12 and 24 months following bariatric surgery compared to baseline ($p < 0.0005$ for both). While the overall effect seemed to be driven by a global change across all brain regions and not from a specific region, our exploratory analysis showed lower delta age in certain brain regions (mainly in somatomotor, visual, and ventral attention networks) at 24 months. This reduced age was also associated with post-surgery improvements in BMI, systolic/diastolic blood pressure, and HOMA-IR (T-value$_{BMI}$ = 4.29, T-value$_{SBP}$ = 4.67, T-value$_{DBP}$ = 4.12, T-value$_{HOMA\text{-}IR}$ = 3.16, all p values < 0.05). In conclusion, these results suggest that obesity-related brain health abnormalities (as measured by delta age) might be reversed by bariatric surgery-induced weight loss and widespread improvements in cardiometabolic alterations.

STRESS

Quantitative mapping of human hair greying and reversal in relation to life stress

Rosenberg, A. M., Rausser, S., Ren, J., Mosharov, E. V., Sturm, G., Ogden, R. T., … Picard, M. (2021). Quantitative mapping of human hair greying and reversal in relation to life stress. *eLife*, *10*, e67437. doi:10.7554/eLife.67437

Abstract

Background: Hair greying is a hallmark of aging generally believed to be irreversible and linked to psychological stress.

Methods: Here, we develop an approach to profile hair pigmentation patterns (HPPs) along individual human hair shafts, producing quantifiable physical timescales of rapid greying transitions.

Results: Using this method, we show white/grey hairs that naturally regain pigmentation across sex, ethnicities, ages, and body regions, thereby quantitatively defining the reversibility of greying in humans. Molecularly, grey hairs upregulate proteins related to energy metabolism, mitochondria, and antioxidant defenses. Combining HPP profiling and proteomics on single hairs, we also report hair greying and reversal that can occur in parallel with psychological stressors. To generalize these observations, we develop a computational simulation, which suggests a threshold-based mechanism for the temporary reversibility of greying.

Conclusions: Overall, this new method to map recent life history quantitatively in HPPs provides an opportunity to examine longitudinally the influence of recent life exposures on human biology.

WELLBEING

Brief structured respiration practices enhance mood and reduce physiological arousal

Balban, M. Y., Neri, E., Kogon, M. M., Weed, L., Nouriani, B., Jo, B., … Huberman, A. D. (2023). Brief structured respiration practices enhance mood and reduce physiological arousal. *Cell Reports Medicine, 4*(1), 100895. doi:10.1016/j.xcrm.2022.100895

Abstract

Controlled breathwork practices have emerged as potential tools for stress management and well-being. Here, we report a remote, randomized, controlled study (NCT05304000) of three different daily 5-minute breathwork exercises compared with an equivalent period of mindfulness meditation over one month. The breathing conditions are (1) cyclic sighing, which emphasizes prolonged exhalations; (2) box breathing, which is equal duration of inhalations, breath retentions, and exhalations; and (3) cyclic hyperventilation with retention, with longer inhalations and shorter exhalations. The primary endpoints are improvement in mood and anxiety as well as reduced physiological arousal (respiratory rate, heart rate, and heart rate variability). Using a mixed-effects model, we show that breathwork, especially the exhale-focused cyclic sighing, produces greater improvement in mood ($p < 0.05$) and reduction in respiratory rate ($p < 0.05$) compared with mindfulness meditation. Daily 5-minute cyclic sighing has promise as an effective stress management exercise.

Is loneliness in emerging adults increasing over time? A preregistered cross-temporal meta-analysis and systematic review

Buecker, S., Mund, M., Chwastek, S., Sostmann, M., & Luhmann, M. (2021). Is loneliness in emerging adults increasing over time? A preregistered cross-temporal meta-analysis and systematic review. *Psychological Bulletin, 147*(8), 787–805. doi:10.1037/bul0000332

Abstract

Judged by the sheer amount of global media coverage, loneliness rates seem to be an increasingly urgent societal concern. From the late 1970s onward, the life experiences of emerging adults have been changing massively due to societal developments such as increased fragmentation of social relationships, greater mobility opportunities, and changes in communication due to technological innovations. These societal developments might have coincided with an increase in loneliness in emerging adults. In the present preregistered cross-temporal meta-analysis, we examined whether loneliness levels in emerging adults have changed over the last 43 years. Our analysis is based on 449 means from 345 studies with 437 independent samples and a total of 124,855 emerging adults who completed the University of California Los Angeles (UCLA) Loneliness Scale between 1976 and 2019. Averaged across all studies, loneliness levels linearly increased with increasing calendar years ($\beta = .224$, 95% CI [.138, .309]). This increase corresponds to 0.56 standard deviations on the UCLA Loneliness Scale over the 43-year studied period. Overall, the results imply that loneliness can be a rising concern in emerging adulthood. Although the frequently used term "loneliness epidemic" seems exaggerated, emerging adults should therefore not be overlooked when designing interventions against loneliness.

Associations of social isolation and loneliness with later dementia

Shen, C., Rolls, E. T., Cheng, W., Kang, J., Dong, G., Xie, C., … Feng, J. (2022). Associations of social isolation and loneliness with later dementia. *Neurology, 99*(2), e164–e175. doi:10.1212/WNL.0000000000200583

Abstract

Objective: To investigate the independent associations of social isolation and loneliness with incident dementia and to explore the potential neurobiological mechanisms.

Methods: We utilized the UK Biobank cohort to establish Cox proportional hazard models with social isolation and loneliness as separate exposures. Demographic (sex, age and ethnicity), socioeconomic (education level, household income and Townsend deprivation index), biological (BMI, APOE genotype, diabetes, cancer, cardiovascular disease and other disabilities), cognitive (speed of processing and visual memory), behavioral (current smoker, alcohol intake and physical activity), and psychological (social isolation or loneliness, depressive symptoms and neuroticism) factors measured at baseline were adjusted. Then, voxel-wise brain-wide association analyses were used to identify gray matter volumes (GMV) associated with social isolation and with loneliness. Partial least squares regression was performed to test the spatial correlation of GMV differences and gene expression using the Allen Human Brain Atlas.

Results: We included 462,619 participants (mean age at baseline 57.0 years [SD 8.1]). With a mean follow-up of 11.7 years (SD 1.7), 4,998 developed all-cause dementia. Social isolation was associated with a 1.26-fold increased risk of dementia (95% CI, 1.15–1.37) independently of various risk factors including loneliness and depression (i.e., full adjustment). However, the fully adjusted hazard ratio for dementia related to loneliness was 1.04 (95% CI, 0.94–1.16); and 75% of this relationship was attributable to depressive symptoms. Structural MRI data were obtained from 32,263 participants (mean age 63.5 years [SD 7.5]). Socially isolated individuals had lower GMVs in temporal, frontal, and other (e.g., hippocampal) regions. Mediation analysis showed that the identified GMVs partly mediated the association between social isolation at baseline and cognitive function at follow-up. Social isolation-related lower GMVs were related to under-expression of genes that are down-regulated in Alzheimer's disease and to genes that are involved in mitochondrial dysfunction and oxidative phosphorylation.

Conclusion: Social isolation is a risk factor for dementia that is independent of loneliness and many other covariates. Social isolation-related brain structural differences coupled with different molecular functions also support the associations of social isolation with cognition and dementia. Social isolation may thus be an early indicator of an increased risk of dementia.

Why people listen: Motivations and outcomes of podcast listening

Tobin, S. J., & Guadagno, R. E. (2022). Why people listen: Motivations and outcomes of podcast listening. *PLoS One*, *17*(4), e0265806. doi:10.1371/journal.pone.0265806

Abstract

The aim of this preregistered study was to identify dispositional predictors of podcast listening and examine the associations between aspects of podcast listening, dispositional predictors, and psychological outcomes. Three hundred and six adults from a range of countries completed an online questionnaire that assessed individual difference predictors (the Big Five personality factors: curiosity, need for cognition, need to belong, age, and gender), aspects of podcast listening (amount, format, setting, device, and social aspects), and potential outcomes (autonomy, competence, relatedness, meaning, mindfulness, and smartphone addiction). As predicted, openness to experience, interest-based curiosity, and need for cognition positively predicted podcast listening. Contrary to predictions, need to belong negatively predicted podcast listening, and time spent listening to podcasts was not associated with autonomy, competence, relatedness, meaning, mindfulness, or smartphone addiction. However, certain aspects of podcast listening (e.g., parasocial relationships and social engagement) were related to positive outcomes and to our predictor variables. Furthermore, neuroticism negatively predicted podcast listening. Overall, the findings support the idea that informational motives can play a role in podcast listening, and that some aspects of listening are associated with positive outcomes.

The avatar will see you now: Support from a virtual human provides socio-emotional benefits

Pauw, L. S., Sauter, D. A., van Kleef, G. A., Lucas, G. M., Gratch, J., & Fischer, A. H. (2022). The avatar will see you now: Support from a virtual human provides socio-emotional benefits. *Computers in Human Behavior*, *136*, 107368. doi:10.1016/j.chb.2022.107368

Abstract

When people are in emotional distress, they often seek support. Virtual humans may provide unique and complementary benefits to human support provision, given that virtual humans are readily available and help sharers overcome socio-evaluative threats, thereby increasing willingness to disclose. Here, we examined whether talking to a virtual human elicits socio-emotional benefits, and whether this is moderated by the type of support provided. To examine the scope of the potential effect, we compared two key types of support (emotional and cognitive), across two emotions (anger and worry). Participants ($N = 115$) shared two personal emotional experiences with a virtual human, who provided either emotional or cognitive support via the Wizard-of-Oz method (i.e., a human-operated avatar). Results showed that participants felt better after talking to the virtual human, as evidenced by reduced intensity of the target emotion and generally improved affect. The emotional improvement was similar for emotional and cognitive support. Cognitive support was also experienced as equally effective as emotional support, and led to similar levels of experienced closeness and desire to interact with the virtual human again. These findings suggest that talking to a virtual human can be a valuable form of support at times of distress.

Predictors of aversion to happiness: New Insights from a multi-national study

Joshanloo, M. (2022). Predictors of aversion to happiness: New Insights from a multi-national study. *Motivation and Emotion*, 1–8. doi:10.1007/s11031-022-09954-1

Abstract
Aversion to happiness is defined as the belief that experiencing or expressing happiness can cause bad things to happen. In this study, the fear of happiness scale was used to measure aversion to happiness in a multinational sample of adults from several countries ($N = 871$). Partial measurement invariance was supported for the fear of happiness scale. The study also examined nine potential predictors of aversion to happiness: gender, age, religiosity, belief in collective happiness, perfectionism, belief in karma, belief in black magic, loneliness, and perception of an unhappy childhood. Bayesian multilevel modeling showed that, except for gender and religiosity, all predictors contributed significantly to the prediction of aversion to happiness. Together, the predictors explained about 28% of the variance in aversion to happiness. The strongest predictors were an unhappy childhood, perfectionism, belief in black magic and karma, and loneliness. This study provides new evidence for the cross-cultural measurement invariance of the fear of happiness scale in adult samples and sheds new light on the nomological network of aversion to happiness.

Happiness comes from trying to make others feel good, rather than oneself

Titova, L., & Sheldon, K. M. (2022). Happiness comes from trying to make others feel good, rather than oneself. *Journal of Positive Psychology, 17*(3), 341–355. doi:10.1080/17439760.2021.1897867

Abstract
Americans are guaranteed the right to 'pursue happiness' for themselves. But might they be better off if they pursued happiness for others? In five studies, we compared the two strategies, showing that, ironically, the second pursuit brings more personal happiness than the first. Retrospective study 1 ($N = 123$) and experimental studies 2 ($N = 96$) and 3 ($N = 141$) show that trying to make someone else happy leads to greater subjective wellbeing than trying to make oneself happy. In all three studies, relatedness need-satisfaction mediated the condition differences. Study 4 ($N = 175$) extended the findings by showing that trying to make others happy is more personally beneficial than when others try to make us happy. Study 5 ($N = 198$) found that feeding strangers' parking meters produced the effect even though the participant did not interact with the targeted other.

Experienced well-being rises with income, even above $75,000 per year

Killingsworth, M. A. (2021). Experienced well-being rises with income, even above $75,000 per year. *Proceedings of the National Academy of Sciences, 118*(4), e2016976118. doi:10.1073/pnas.2016976118

Abstract
What is the relationship between money and well-being? Research distinguishes between two forms of well-being: people's feelings during the moments of life (experienced well-being) and people's evaluation of their lives when they pause and reflect (evaluative well-being). Drawing on 1,725,994 experience-sampling reports from 33,391 employed US adults, the present results show that both experienced and evaluative well-being increased linearly

with log(income), with an equally steep slope for higher earners as for lower earners. There was no evidence for an experienced well-being plateau above $75,000/year, contrary to some influential past research. There was also no evidence of an income threshold at which experienced and evaluative well-being diverged, suggesting that higher incomes are associated with both feeling better day-to-day and being more satisfied with life overall.

The fatiguing effects of camera use in virtual meetings: A within-person field experiment

Shockley, K. M., Gabriel, A. S., Robertson, D., Rosen, C. C., Chawla, N., Ganster, M. L., & Ezerins, M. E. (2021). The fatiguing effects of camera use in virtual meetings: A within-person field experiment. *Journal of Applied Psychology, 106*(8), 1137–1155. doi:10.1037/apl0000948

Abstract

The COVID-19 pandemic propelled many employees into remote work arrangements, and face-to-face meetings were quickly replaced with virtual meetings. This rapid uptick in the use of virtual meetings led to much popular press discussion of virtual meeting fatigue (i.e., "Zoom fatigue"), described as a feeling of being drained and lacking energy following a day of virtual meetings. In this study, we aimed to better understand how one salient feature of virtual meetings—the camera—impacts fatigue, which may affect outcomes during meetings (e.g., participant voice and engagement). We did so through the use of a 4-week within-person experience sampling field experiment where camera use was manipulated. Drawing from theory related to self-presentation, we propose and test a model where study condition (camera on versus off) was linked to daily feelings of fatigue; daily fatigue, in turn, was presumed to relate negatively to voice and engagement during virtual meetings. We further predict that gender and organizational tenure will moderate this relationship such that using a camera during virtual meetings will be more fatiguing for women and newer members of the organization. Results of 1,408 daily observations from 103 employees supported our proposed model, with supplemental analyses suggesting that fatigue affects same-day and next-day meeting performance. Given the anticipated prevalence of remote work even after the pandemic subsides, our study offers key insights for ongoing organizational best practices surrounding virtual meetings.

Cannabis use does not increase actual creativity but biases evaluations of creativity

Heng, Y. T., Barnes, C. M., & Yam, K. C. (2022). Cannabis use does not increase actual creativity but biases evaluations of creativity. *Journal of Applied Psychology, 108*(4), 635–646. doi:10.1037/apl0000599

Abstract

In this research, we examine the effects of cannabis use on creativity and evaluations of creativity. Drawing on both the broaden-and-build theory and the affect-as-information model, we propose that cannabis use would facilitate more creativity as well as more favorable evaluations of creativity via cannabis-induced joviality. We tested this prediction in two experiments, wherein participants were randomly assigned to either a cannabis use or cannabis abstinence condition. We find support for our prediction that cannabis use facilitates joviality, which translates to more favorable evaluations of creativity of one's own ideas and others' ideas. However, our prediction that cannabis use facilitates creativity via joviality was not supported. Our findings suggest that cannabis use may positively bias evaluations of creativity but have no impact on creativity. Implications for theory and practice are discussed.

Microdosing with psilocybin mushrooms: A double-blind placebo-controlled study

Cavanna, F., Muller, S., de la Fuente, L. A., Zamberlan, F., Palmucci, M., Janeckova, L., … Tagliazucchi, E. (2022). Microdosing with psilocybin mushrooms: A double-blind placebo-controlled study. *Translational Psychiatry, 12*(1), 307. doi:10.1038/s41398-022-02039-0

Abstract

The use of low sub-perceptual doses of psychedelics ("microdosing") has gained popularity in recent years. Although anecdotal reports claim multiple benefits associated with this practice, the lack of placebo-controlled studies severely limits our knowledge of microdosing and its effects. Moreover, research conducted in standard laboratory settings could fail to capture the motivation of individuals engaged or planning to engage in microdosing protocols, thus underestimating the likelihood of positive effects on creativity and cognitive function. We recruited 34 individuals starting to microdose with psilocybin mushrooms (*Psilocybe cubensis*), one of the materials most frequently used for this purpose. Following a double-blind placebo-controlled experimental design, we investigated the acute and short-term effects of 0.5 g of dried mushrooms on subjective experience, behavior, creativity (divergent and convergent thinking), perception, cognition, and brain activity. The reported acute effects were significantly more intense for the active dose compared to the placebo, but only for participants who correctly identified their experimental condition. These changes were accompanied by reduced EEG power in the theta band, together with preserved levels of Lempel-Ziv broadband signal complexity. For all other measurements there was no effect of microdosing except for few small changes toward cognitive impairment. According to our findings, low doses of psilocybin mushrooms can result in noticeable subjective effects and altered EEG rhythms, but without evidence to support enhanced wellbeing, creativity, and cognitive function. We conclude that expectation underlies at least some of the anecdotal benefits attributed to microdosing with psilocybin mushrooms.

www.ingramcontent.com/pod-product-compliance
Lightning Source LLC
LaVergne TN
LVHW082358200926
848481LV00012B/3607
9781604151756